EASY IN HARNESS

A PRODUCTIVE APPROACH TO HIRING A GOOD MANAGER

ALAN J. COHEN

atmosphere press

Published by Atmosphere Press

Cover design by Felipe Betim
Cover illustration from the painting "Sanctuary" ©2023 by Anita Sison Cohen catalog #Y2023N001-391

Atmospherepress.com

PRAISE FOR *EASY IN HARNESS*

"[W]ith...acute powers of observation...Cohen plunges in from page one, with short tales of people who have been moved to retire, change professions, and in some cases, endure, in a situation involving poor management... [He] has constructed a fascinating, lengthy Case Study chapter in which he contrasts and compares the autocratic and entrepreneurial styles as seen...in a large pharmaceutical company, illustrating the step-by-step development of these two vastly different approaches... He then highlights the efforts and successes of entrepreneurs Ben and Jerry, who started small and ultimately spread their tasty products across the nation...to embody the true entrepreneurial model... [He] presents material diligently gathered and well-organized... One quality that will satisfy his readers is his persistent use of female leadership examples, on both sides of the scale he has created, which will make his stated thesis even more attractive to a wide readership.... Cohen's exploration... is both educational and entertaining and is clearly based on long career experience."

— **Barbara Bamberger Scott,** *Feathered Quill*

"I just finished reading Dr. Cohen's concise and important book.... I heartily recommend that any MD who is about to undertake a management position or who will be working directly with a non-physician manager in their practice or academic department should spend some time reading this very worthwhile text. It will be time well spent... Very, very few physicians have experience in management... Dr. Cohen's short book fills this knowledge gap admirably."

— **Joseph S. Alpert, MD, Professor of Medicine, University of Arizona College of Medicine, Tucson, AZ; editor in chief, The American Journal of Medicine**

To Anita Sison Cohen
genius, muse, and wife
who inspires
reads and revises
and sustains me

Table of Contents

Career vs. Mission

Inspiration of Respect, Trust, and Confidence (RTC)

Communication Skills

What Employers Need to Know: Hiring from Above

A Broader Context

Preface

Apparently without design, fortune has furnished me with a varied education in the categories and hierarchies of labor. I have been a manual laborer, a day laborer, summer help, a camp counselor, and a rank and file employee; a physician in many settings; a teacher at five different institutions, a manager of teachers and an associate program director (responsible for training medical residents); a business owner, managing the accounting, marketing and financial management myself, drawing on an innate predisposition supplemented by appropriate college courses. For ten years I managed medical clinics, in charge of as many as 200 employees responsible for 25,000 clients; and have twice been an administrator. Both as employee and as manager, I have worked for excellent, good, adequate, and terrible bosses. Though I have never been a member of a union, I have spent more than twenty years working beside and managing members, once during a prolonged strike, and I was the president of an employee executive committee representing seventy physicians with administration. I have been fascinated by leadership since childhood (perhaps in part because my father was a superintendent of schools, but also in part as a result of defending vulnerable classmates from bullies on the playground during recess), and I completed a competitive and rigorous two-year executive leadership program.

It was only lately, however, toward the end of my career,

that I came to a full appreciation of the phenomenon that I plan to address here. It has grown increasingly distinct and evident as others' questions, complaints, comments, and analyses, superimposed upon my own embryonic experiences, readings, and insights, began to settle themselves into a coherent message. Since they have, it has become a growing preoccupation as I have grown increasingly aware that it is a critical issue that seems to be neglected, to fly below the radar. Why is this not a cause célèbre, I have wondered, a national topic of conversation? It so clearly stands at the center of our culture and has such vast implications.

As intuition evolved into conviction, I felt compelled to share my insight and do it justice. I no longer have any doubt about the accuracy of my analysis—I only hope that I can muster sufficient cogency and eloquence that you will begin to feel my sense of urgency. So much seems to be at stake, and it is difficult to alter vested interests and enduring preconceptions.

If you have ever had the good fortune to see a truly happy and productive workplace, you will never want to go back to *business as usual.* If you have had the even greater fortune to have had a part in building such a department, you may read this book with a sense of recognition and enjoyment—it will perhaps help you to appreciate and categorize what you already know. However, if you have never seen such an ideal workplace, you may well find the descriptions of it I have provided farfetched, exaggerated, or frankly fantastic. Still, if I have done my job well enough, the recipe for building them is here in this manuscript. It really is simply a matter of hiring and nurturing the right kind of leadership.

What Employees Know: A View of Management from Below

– 1 –

Retiring

My best friend, whom I've known since I was seven, made a close friend during his first week in college in Connecticut. After graduation, this college friend turned down two Ivy League law schools to start a career at a Fortune Fifty company. He rose slowly up the corporate ladder, spending time in several areas of the business along the way; and he developed a particular expertise in the field of executive compensation. After more than twenty years of relative success, a brilliant young executive, new to the firm, selected him to build the global operational capability the firm lacked. She was the first manager he had who, as he puts it, "Recognized my skills and passion, and gave me the opportunity and the support to pursue a vital challenge for the firm." He excelled in this role and built a highly effective organization that succeeded beyond expectations. However, this supportive young manager died prematurely, and, at nearly the same time, her boss, the executive officer of this corporate staff, retired. Where the former chief officer, a tough ex-marine, was demanding and led through positive reinforcement and encouragement of his management team, his successor employed intimidation and threats, and adapted the young woman's successor to this approach. After several years under this new management style, the college friend realized that he would never be able to accomplish what he wished to accomplish in this environment and retired after thirty-two years of service, though he had previously planned to work there for another ten years. In his words, leaving is something he would never have done had the management in the original firm "not converted a successful, collaborative environment where everyone was willing to be accountable for their actions, into one that felt so predatory and risk-filled, where creativity was squelched, and the best leaders chose to leave the firm at a much higher rate."

– 2 –

Changing Professions

My sister-in-law studied for five years to become a food technologist. What she learned was primarily chemistry bench research: in particular, how to develop and modify flavors and how to improve food industry gums. She was really good at this, was getting incrementally better, and she loved to do it. She then had six jobs in food technology over a period of twenty years, where she utilized these skills. Her employers all raved about her. She was industrious and inventive. She achieved many useful discoveries and modifications, helping her employers to flourish. Her evaluations were uniformly outstanding. However, her managers wanted her, more as the years passed, to meet with customers and market the products she was developing, often asking her to misrepresent the stage of development or the certainty of a result. She did as she was asked, of course, with sufficient success to satisfy her bosses, but she had no training in sales, nor was it something she wanted to do. "Work was never fun," she says now. And so, this highly successful food technologist with twenty years' experience and the kind of work ethic employers cherish, left food technology and took up accounting instead. Fifteen years later, she feels she made the right decision changing over; although accounting has its own challenges, it has proved to be a better fit. Still, she did love the bench work she was trained to do. She would have stayed on, probably helped some company prosper, perhaps identified new flavors, contributed to the development of her field, and perhaps helped to train young food technologists if she had worked for an entrepreneurial manager. She would have responded to support as a dry plant does to rain, to someone who leveraged her training, empowered her, and let the sales staff sell the products she developed.

– 3 –

Leaving to Work for Competitors

In my forties, I worked for six years at an Ivy League University health plan, caring for students and employees and their families: cooks, bottle washers, and professors emeriti. I was one of four doctors hired in a six-month period to replace some departures and help expand the primary care department to accommodate an increase in the size of the University staff. For the first five years, we did what we had been hired to do enthusiastically. We got along well together, among ourselves and with the rest of the staff; our patients received high-quality care and were happy with us, and we enjoyed our work.

We also taught students and residents and were involved in a variety of valued academic activities. Highly motivated, we did not need much encouragement. Our manager admitted that he did not like patient care and said that he was intentionally *user unfriendly* when it came to night call coverage, but in his role in our department that did little harm.

Then the Health Plan director was promoted into an entirely unrelated chain of command, and the position thereby vacated remained open for eighteen months. In the end, after two national searches, our department chair became the new director. Unfortunately, the atmosphere changed with the management; collegiality gave way to tension, and support for workers melted away. The new director did not choose to capitalize on the search for a computer system that had already been completed to make his mark. (A team of ten health plan employees, after a two-year search of five medical records computing systems already in use at other institutions, had recommended the purchase of a system that had demonstrated substantial improvements in quality, safety and cost, but clinical computing was not introduced at the Health Plan for another five or ten years.) Instead, although access had not been a significant concern, he chose to introduce open access to the health plan and invited consultants to oversee the introduction. Suddenly, no employee's opinion seemed to matter anymore. An atmosphere of secrecy descended like a curtain. Arbitrary and capricious new rules and expectations were introduced. Over the next eighteen months, six of the nine primary care doctors working at the Health Plan moved to new jobs. One became a superstar at a nearby hospital: founding director of a residency program, editor of a journal, author of books and journal articles, columnist, and candidate for Surgeon General. Another eventually became the Director of Public Health for a state in New England. Our best work was still ahead of all of us. But if the management at the University Health Plan had accommodated us, we might have done our best work there, and gone on providing our patients with the continuity of care they were beginning to enjoy again with us; and our transitions to new positions might have been mutually agreed upon and collegial, diminishing the turmoil involved in job search, job change, and moving, and in the hiring of new employees.

A year later, one of the doctors who stayed on had the opportunity to see the consultants' report. It recommended ignoring the opinion of the doctors who worked there and suggested in so many words that, if they did not go along with the plans laid down for change, they be let go. The turnover continued to exceed the national average for primary care providers. And although employee dissatisfaction with him persists, the same manager was publicly praised and reappointed ten years later and remains in place now after more than twenty years. The son of a provider still working at the Health Plan called last week for an appointment with his provider for an acute problem. Though they had a full complement of staff, he was told that the first available appointment was ten days away. Prior to the initiative to improve access, when we all worked there, no one had to wait that long to see us.

– 4 –
Staying On—1

Though idiosyncratic in their details, these vignettes are prototypes, dishearteningly prevalent and poignant illustrations of some of the costs of flawed leadership. Employees leave, join competitors, even abandon the profession in which they'd trained to work; and they retire prematurely. Not everyone, though, has the resources, energy, or intrepidity to choose such healthy, if disruptive, alternatives. Imperfect management is almost certainly even more stressful for those who stay. However, the impact of their workplace on employees who spend their working lives under stress, who feel, for example, unappreciated, fearful, abused, or threatened, is harder to quantify. Millions of employees cope with such stresses, but the coping capacities and stresses vary so much from one employee to another, and from one workplace to another they are difficult to study. Still, the studies that do exist suggest substantial mental and physical harm; and, of course, we all know people who have been in such circumstances. We know they can predispose to anxiety, depression, sleeplessness, excessive use of drugs or alcohol, smoking, excessive weight, family tensions, anger and emotional breakdowns. Such chronic stress is felt to predispose to posttraumatic stress disorder (PTSD) in as many as one-third of those exposed. And inevitably, such workplaces may also contribute to acting out: to divorce, criminal behavior, suicide, or homicide.

Let's ask an employee who has stayed on for a year in a workplace with a new dysfunctional manager to describe his experience for you. "How does it feel to be an employee in such an environment?"

"I have always looked on the bright side," he says.

My coworkers tell me, "You are too trusting." Recently though, I haven't felt as trusting as I used to. It's hard to trust people who lie to you and don't bother to keep track of their lies. Last week, my manager told me she was as frustrated as I was at not getting a raise this year. Then yesterday she let it slip out she'd bought a house with the raise they told her about last month. That's none of my business either way, but it supports my notion that either she'd rather lie than tell the truth or she's sworn to secrecy; and that she finds it too much trouble to even remember just who I am and what she's said to me. She does have her favorites, spies my coworkers call them, but I'm definitely not one of them. They take forty-five-minute lunches and put me on report if I'm five seconds late in the morning. I used to be proud of what I did and praised for it too. I used to enjoy coming to work every day, having lunch in the day room, even going to meetings. Meetings now are scary and sometimes depressing. They usually involve threats or blame and new projects that require our commitment but then somehow never get off the ground.

I come to work now because I have to make ends meet, period. There's nothing to be proud of anymore. We're less productive than we were five years ago. Many of the coworkers I used to look forward to seeing are gone, and a lot of them have changed. They're quiet or angry, or morose. Nowadays, all the talk is about management—how dumb they are, how badly they treat us: like slaves, we are, or prisoners. I don't like that kind of talk—it's not productive and my mom used to say that saying things can make them come true. But I can't help thinking they're right. I don't feel useful anymore. I'm not contributing. It's like cleaning toilets or mucking out the barn for a rich and nasty boss who abuses you and holds back your pay. Sometimes I hate coming to work. Sometimes I take a mental health day in self-defense. Nearly everyone else does too. Everything is negative here. There's all this hoopla and misinformation about how great the company is and all it's doing. But our stock price is way down, and we aren't growing anymore. We never seem to fix problems when they are first pointed out. We wait until they become a crisis and we have to do something. But by then it's usually too late.

You know what I think? I've started to think that the new administrators were hired to destroy the business. I heard that the owners need a tax break and they want to sell to our competitors. They are such sticklers for rules. They make a big fuss about how many pens we use, and they buy a car for the new boss. It takes the heart out of you. I honestly don't care anymore. I'm short with customers, and I'm short with coworkers. And no one cares. I don't think this can go on. So many people have left; and the few who have come to replace them are mostly "yes" men, too green and too busy kowtowing to help much with what needs to get done. Everyone's gaining weight and smoking, no one gets any exercise, and there's an epidemic of diabetes. And we are at each other's throats. Simple, important things aren't getting done. I'd leave myself if I could find another job. I'd even take a cut in pay. You don't have any suggestions, do you? No one here helps anymore. They don't even listen. Too busy talking about their own problems...their own fear...their own anger. Like me.

These comments reflect what an average worker in a dysfunctional contemporary workplace often feels: trapped, anxious, and trying to make sense of the experience. Such employees often have difficulty articulating just what is wrong, but being in such situations leaves scars. Of course, the susceptibility of employees varies; so does their treatment. Some escape the worst of the trauma and abuse. Yet nearly everyone emerges, if and when such a regime changes, less willing to trust, less willing to take chances, less willing to say what they really think, less participatory, inventive, enthusiastic, less willing to join a team, less supportive of other employees, less optimistic.

– 5 –

Staying On—2

Chronic stress predisposes to physical symptoms as well—to skin rashes, headache, abdominal pain and/or loss of appetite or overeating, constipation, diarrhea, fatigue, restlessness, nausea, muscle tightness, asthma, shortness of breath, palpitations, tremors, sweating, choking, difficulty swallowing, and the like. These symptoms result in more frequent medical office and emergency room visits, so testing and medication use occasion increased healthcare costs and side effects. And there is what I would call good objective evidence that such stress causes a vicious cycle of high blood pressure, heart disease, stroke and death; while somewhat less robust evidence suggests that work stress may well also predispose to various cancers.

It may help to have a global statistical picture of the possible impact of such stress. More than 155 million people work as employees in this country, about one-half the population. Most of them are employed in established workplaces and so potentially subject to the daily influence of the kinds of managers we have begun to consider. Last year, 2% of men and 5% of women had PTSD. Sometime during their lives, 5% of men and 10% of women have PTSD, and 30% of men and 26% of women who have served in the armed forces have PTSD. Clearly, sufficient stress can multiply the risk of PTSD three to six times. If workplace stress doubles the risk, it could be responsible for the occurrence of PTSD in some two million workers. Depression is just about twice as common as PTSD.

Our workforce is also aging. Between 2000 and 2010, the number of workers over fifty-five grew by 65% while the number under fifty-five grew by less than 2%, and this trend is expected to continue. By 2010, sixty-six million workers were over forty-five. As older workers are at the greatest risk of heart disease, that risk is growing rapidly for workers in stressful workplaces. Twenty-five percent of the population has hypertension, 10% has heart disease, and 4% has had a heart attack. Studies suggest that workplace stress increases hypertension and heart attacks with risk for either increased by 50%. Workplace stress may well be responsible for seven million cases of hypertension, perhaps a million heart attacks and 100,000 deaths from heart attacks each year.

So employees who stay on in difficult workplaces may be at substantial risk. They often feel trapped and suffer from nonspecific symptoms, have problems with interpersonal relationships, or become ill.

– 6 –

Managing

Good ends, as I have frequently to point out, can be achieved only by the employment of appropriate means. The end cannot justify the means, for the simple and obvious reason that the means employed determine the nature of the ends produced.
— Ends and Means, Aldous Huxley

Still, it might be objected, don't these worker complaints just represent special pleading? Of course, everyone prefers comfort and security. But isn't stress necessary to achieve productivity? Don't workers require discipline? Isn't a little fear salutary? Isn't the collateral damage described so far—job change, psychosomatic complaints, even heart attacks—inevitable, part of the necessary cost of doing business?

In fact, the opposite is almost certainly true: all this damage is not only unnecessary, but it actually reduces employee productivity and makes business success markedly less likely for organizations that promote *bad* managers. Enlightened management is the bedrock on which the sustained success of any company is built.

The Crucial Management Dilemma

– 7 –

Enlightened Management—Entrepreneurial, not Autocratic

> If you use laws to direct the people, and punishments to control them, they will merely try to evade the punishments and will have no sense of shame. But if by virtue you guide them, and by the rites you control them, there will be a sense of shame and right.
> — Analects, Confucius

And so we have arrived at the crucial question on which all else depends: what constitutes enlightened management? To put it another way, if success in business depends on productivity, and management exists to optimize productivity, what kind of management will deliver the greatest productivity? The question has haunted our workplaces for generations. Properly considered, it is a question that plumbs the depths of what it means to be human. The subject has certainly been approached from many perspectives: there are countless surveys of workers and managers; there are numerous articles and books. Nearly all have arrived at multifactorial explanations and are circumspect in their conclusions or frankly fatalistic.

Yet despite all this industry, there is no accepted guideline that reliably identifies what is problematic and what works. What makes a bad manager ineffective and a good manager successful? How do we optimize productivity?

Over the years, it has become increasingly clear to me that there is only one issue central to effective management: is a manager authoritarian or entrepreneurial? If you come to agree, it will be a first step on the road to choosing from among various candidates the managers you want to hire. So I will further define these two fundamental management styles; address pertinent social and psychological forces and consider how they make each approach more or less attractive; discuss four other vital aspects of good management; examine management styles in the context of an actual workplace; consider various theoretical models; and provide detailed and specific suggestions for hiring good managers.

– 8 –

Definitions

Autocracy needs little introduction. Kings, oligarchs, and dictators are autocrats; we in America have demonstrated a preference, at least in our politics, for democracy. Autocracy in the workplace is management by the exercise of power. In return for their pay, workers submit to the will of their leaders. Though we will be reviewing some of the implications in the coming pages, most of us are quite familiar with them already.

Because democracy is not a viable option in the workplace, if we do not desire autocracy, we must identify another option. In this book I am proposing entrepreneurship as that option.

Though perhaps a less familiar concept in the workplace, entrepreneurship and how it differs from autocracy will be a recurrent theme for us. We can begin our inquiry here by observing that, while an autocrat coerces and threatens, an entrepreneur encourages and promotes. Clearly, these means are diametrically opposed, and they reflect attitudes toward management and human nature that have far-reaching consequences; and, I hope to demonstrate to your satisfaction, ends that are equally disparate.

Entrepreneur is a relatively new word. Though coined in the 1400s to mean undertaking an activity, it had fallen into relative disuse for centuries. It was only resurrected around 1730 by Richard Cantillon (and at that point only in French) in his groundbreaking Essai, to mean anyone, essentially any merchant—butcher, baker, farmer, wine dealer, master artisan and the like. The Oxford English Dictionary still considered the word entrepreneur obsolete in the 1930s. In retrospect, though, it was probably first used in English to connote business ownership in the second half of the nineteenth century; though our present emphasis on innovation, risk, and energy was only added well into the twentieth century. The word's root is *prize*, meaning *lever*; the French verb still means to attempt, try, adventure, to take responsibility for. To be enterprising captures the gist in English; it now implies flexibility, energy, invention, complete immersion in the mission, and a willingness to take risks. It has, of course, been used to denominate individuals who develop new businesses but, because these traits infrequently apply to such individuals, who more often turn out to be predators than innovators or risk takers, I have chosen for this book to use the term impresario for the managers of startups and the term *entrepreneur* exclusively for the innovative, open, flexible style of management we are examining. (James Surowiecki, *The New Yorker*, Vol 85 #45 1/18/2010: 24-29.)

(Webster's New World Dictionary has it that an entrepreneur

is "a person who organizes and manages a business undertaking, assuming the risk for the sake of the profit." However, in my experience, an entrepreneurial manager takes the risk for the sake of the challenge and sees his pay check as a pleasant but secondary concern. While in their private lives, entrepreneurs are as partial to money as their fellow men [though rarely obsessed], profit for the organization is the mission, and so the goal; but, once embarked, the only meaningful reward is success and, within reason, everything else is sacrificed, even, if necessary, at least for a time, personal profit. In fact, though it is counterproductive to take advantage of this circumstance, some entrepreneurial leaders would pay to do jobs they find attractive and do, at times, take cuts in pay to take advantage of unusual opportunities to learn or to immerse themselves in new experience, even when that may not advance their careers.)

Enterprise and adventure suggest another dimension to entrepreneurial ethos—it is attractive, can even be fun. Sadly, in general, work and play are considered antonyms, but an entrepreneurial workplace is often one that workers look forward to coming to in the morning and do not want to leave at night. The upshot is that, by design, an entrepreneur creates an invigorating workplace and an autocrat a somber one. The entrepreneur leverages the collective invention and energy of all her workers to optimize productivity, using encouragement within a carefully structured environment, while the autocrat uses threat and punishment to force workers to optimize productivity.

Social Forces

– 9 –

Motivation

So which is better: to provide discipline and inspire fear or to encourage creativity and foster safety? Which of these approaches, which of these environments, is the more productive? In my estimation, although most management theory and training promotes empowerment, hiring favors the autocrat, so that somewhere between three in five and four in five managers are autocrats, whether covertly or openly, significantly outnumbering entrepreneurs. But which one provides better outcomes?

Since there are no definitive experiments, and since impeccably controlled experiments may not, in fact, be possible, it may prove useful to start with thought experiments. You may believe, as Rousseau did, that man, in a state of nature, is altruistic, or like Hobbes, that he is self-interested, but what can we expect as an outcome if we cleave hard-headedly to the bottom line? Are happy workers more productive? We know that a modicum of anxiety can be a goad to production, but its efficacy tends to depend upon the source of the anxiety. Sufficient anxiety might well be created by worry about failure;

while when salutary anxiety spills over into fear or anger, as it inevitably does in autocratic workplaces, the losses may be greater than the gains.

What seems likely to work and why? Which principles govern the behavior of employees in the workplace? What elicits resistance? What creates loyalty? What motivates a worker to give his best, to come early, stay late, enjoy work, treat customers not only with respect but with enthusiasm, and want to deliver to your organization the kind of energy an Olympic basketball player will devote to rebounding or passing?

– 10 –

Dictatorship

Education makes a people easy to lead, but difficult to drive; easy to govern, but impossible to enslave.
—Henry, Baron Brougham

We can begin by considering the nature of our society. What unique challenges face American workplaces? What is the context? What is the mindset of the worker we employ? First, the United States is a participatory democracy. We have universal suffrage and universal education. Our citizens are encouraged to learn about government, to attend caucuses, vote, and contact their representatives to express their opinions. The assumption at the base of this participation is that the people are wise, that those who are governed should not only have representation but actually know what is best, choose well, and should have the power to decide their fate. And so far this democracy seems to have worked and made us the most powerful and successful nation on Earth.

The workplace, though, is a dictatorship. And, while most employees accept the need for a single controlling intelligence to manage work activities, they do so with reservations. They want a benign dictator, someone who will be fair; someone who will seek his opinion, consider it carefully and communicate decisions and the reasons for them in a timely and understandable manner; someone who will lead the team to success and reward those who helped to achieve that success. A vast preponderance of employees start out wanting to use their skills, to contribute to a successful team, to work hard for a common meaningful goal under enlightened support and interactive leadership; and they expect to participate, to be a part of the conversation, to be represented in the mission, vision, and values, in the products and services of the organization. When that does not happen, frustration, resistance, and hostility often ensue. It may not always be a conscious process, but the workplace dictator's employees measure the dictator's performance; and they produce according to their evaluation, stinting where they feel he falls short of their notion of an ideal leader.

– 11 –

Independence

Courage my Lord, proceeds from self-dependence;
Teach man to think he's a free agent,
Give but a slave his liberty, he'll shake
Off sloth, and build himself a hut, and hedge
A spot of ground; this he'll defend; 'tis his

> By right of nature: thus set in action,
> He will still move onward.
> —Edward III, William Blake

American citizens have unalienable rights to life, liberty, and the pursuit of happiness. They have an entire Bill of Rights, amendments to the constitution, and have, in particular, their rights of free speech and assembly. And there are rights related specifically to the workplace: for example, the right to unionize (National Labor Relations Act, 1935) and to be free of harassment and discrimination (Title VII of the Civil Rights Act, 1964). Children (and many adults), when they feel their enthusiasm curbed by disagreement or resistance, will say, "It's a free country," and mean, I can do whatever I want as long as it is not blatantly hurtful to others.

Employees expect their rights to be respected in the workplace and are aggrieved when they feel they are not. Recourse to remedies is often difficult, but they may feel betrayed whenever they detect any least failure to adhere to the reciprocal responsibilities they instinctively cherish, whenever they feel disrespected or ill-treated, according not only to the letter but also to the intent of the law of the land; and they behave accordingly. The entrepreneur's tendency to engage with employees can communicate respect for rights and so minimize wasteful confrontation.

– 12 –

Expectations

The American media report on a wide variety of sensational events. Most involve actions that exceed expectations, break laws, or ignore limits. They often involve the lives of the rich and famous: royalty, inheritors of wealth, tycoons, sports stars, stars of the silver screen, teen singing idols, and charismatic, innovative, relentless, or daring criminals (often admiringly called outlaws). Moreover, most fictional popular culture, from comic books to romance novels, from rock and hip-hop music to Hollywood movies, from *Breaking Bad* to reality TV, help to create irrational outsized expectations, self-aggrandizement, and feelings of personal inadequacy. Workers often have personal knowledge of individuals who have *made good* or *gotten away with murder* and are enjoying the extraordinary rewards of income and recognition that accompany such success. Such evidence of the rewards of capitalism can create unreasonable expectations among susceptible individuals.

In addition, particularly since the 1960s, affluent parenting has been characterized by more indulgence and less discipline than had been the norm earlier. Children have been provided with resources and encouragement to find and express themselves. They are, regardless of merit, commonly used to positive feedback, permissive parents, helicopter or soccer moms, chauffeurs, enrichment, high expectations, but indulgence when they fail; and feel entitled to a succession of options and new opportunities.

On the other hand, many raised in penury have become accustomed to abuse and neglect, poverty of experience, negative feedback, inadequate nutrition and/or lack of sleep, failure of confidence, and may learn to cope by evasion, deception, and/ or make-believe.

Clearly our culture and upbringing are not calculated to develop ideal employees. But it is equally clear that they make discipline and exclusion from decision-making less likely to succeed than they might in many other cultures.

– 13 –

Totalitarianism

When the bio-social pendulum swings away from active
cooperation towards tyranny, the whole society becomes corrupt.
It may shift 4,883,000 tons of stone to build a pyramid; but with
its deformed social structure its days are numbered.
—The Human Zoo, Desmond Morris

The example of other cultures, however, also tends to reinforce the prejudices of our potential employees. Countries that
have adopted coercive models in the recent past have created
atrocities, abuses, crimes against humanity and displaced or
removed large parts of their populations from productive
activity altogether. The methods employed, as described by
historians, are surprisingly similar to those of managers in
coercive workplaces. The messages imparted by governance
in Nazi Germany and Communist China, the Soviet Union and
Communist Eastern Europe are primarily warnings about the
abuse of power. The superiority of capitalism takes a back
seat in the popular imagination to that of democracy and the
rule of law. In any case, what capitalism means to workers, as
consumers, is lots of choices, low prices, special discounts, the
option to return items, and "the customer is always right," at
least when they are customers. What they generally do understand about the theory of capitalism is that greed, everyone
following her or his own inclinations, pursuing his or her
interests, is supposed to create more wealth than organized
effort (whether or not that is actually true), and that competition and ferment are creative. None of that, however, makes
them any more willing to work long hours at low wages to

increase an owner's profits.

Workers are also aware of how Toyota involved employees in innovation and so of the concept that workers know best about how to optimize their own productivity; and that idea has, of course, been imported. Total Quality Management (TQM) in the 1990s became Systems Redesign in the 2000s, and so the concept of teams of front-line employees meeting to define processes and resolve problems has filtered into the consciousness of workers, often through personal experience.

– 14 –

Dominance

So far it may seem that managers planning to exploit discipline and fear are working against much in our culture, and, in all likelihood, against much in human nature as well. They do have at least one vigorous potential ally, though, as Erich Fromm's *Escape from Freedom* makes clear: the worker himself. He suggests that we are all dependent in childhood; then, generally, sometime in our teens, we all become independent or free. This freedom, however, is accompanied by an aloneness and powerlessness so severe that each of us is driven to form new relationships. As Fromm says:

> *two courses are open to him....He can relate himself spontaneously to the world in love and work, in the genuine expression of his emotional, sensuous, and intellectual capacities; he can thus become one again with man, nature, and himself, without giving up the*

independence and integrity of his individual self. The other course open to him is to fall back, to give up his freedom....This course of escape...is also characterized by the more or less complete surrender of individuality and the integrity of the self....it does not solve the underlying problem and is paid for by a kind of life that often consists only of automatic or compulsive behaviors.

The dominance of the strong, and the submission of those who feel insignificant and/or powerless, is common in the workplace. It can also be, though unhealthy, reasonably productive. With its primary goal of exploitation and its deceptive practical harmony of interest, it seems, at first glance, to be an ideal approach to productivity. But it is useful to recall that it is the same kind of social system that underlay and subsidized the South before the Civil War, Nazi Germany, and the USSR. What they have in common, of course, is that they were all defeated by more nurturing, open, democratic societies. Once again, these are not controlled trials, and the explanation for victory in any war is multifactorial; but the analogy is certainly suggestive.

On the other hand, promoting growth, independence and integrity, and encouraging freedom, can release an appreciation and energy powerful enough to overcome any obstacle and conquer any challenge. The entrepreneur can, without exploitation, not only help each employee to grow into her best self but also contribute in a healthy and vigorous fashion to the enterprise she leads.

– 15 –

Behaviorism

An autocrat also draws on a rich vein of behaviorism, the scientific theory of psychology that arose and evolved in America in the early twentieth century. For centuries men and women, by trial and error, have domesticated animals and trained them to fetch and roll over, jump fences, run races, and even count. Observation and experiment created a science of such control, beginning with Pavlov's stimulus-response dogs, salivating at the anticipation of food induced by the bell that was only a precursor to its arrival, and extending through the identification of learning curves and the use of reward and punishment to submission/dominance relationships and hierarchies of authority. As the scientists' sophistication grew, B.F. Skinner formulated a model, which he called operant conditioning, probably the most advanced manifestation of the movement. The operant is the behavior the scientist wants to encourage; the characteristic experiment involved an animal in a cage encouraged by the positive reinforcement of food (or by the negative reinforcement of electric shock) to do the thing desired more often.

Operant conditioning clearly works: it can elicit a variety of desired responses. An autocrat who chooses to encourage habits of obedience and then habits of workday behavior deemed likely to optimize productivity is supported by this scientific enterprise. If work involved only rote tasks—carrying buckets, unloading trucks, adding columns of figures, performing one task over and over on an assembly line—if there were no need for human interaction and no need for change or improvement, developing habits of obedience would be nearly as effective as building robots to do the tasks. However, there are few rote jobs anymore; and it can be reductive, demeaning, and counterproductive to treat people as one might dogs or horses or hawks—or machines.

When employees agree to work for employers, they implicitly give their consent to have management exercise authority over them. How they are managed determines whether this consent is voluntary, as it is when they join an organization and elect officers, or involuntary, as it is when they are drafted into the military. Management has a right and a responsibility to exercise power. Behaviorism provides us with useful insight into pertinent animal and human behavior. However, using that power and that insight effectively will generally involve encouraging employees to give their consent to management's power over them voluntarily and, whenever possible, enthusiastically.

– 16 –

Psychology

For Zeus almighty takes half the good
Out of a man on the day he becomes a slave.
—Homer (tr. Stephen Mitchell)

Still the best argument is based on individual psychology. In any society, at any time, if you are interested in getting the best efforts from employees, you must win their hearts and minds. An enthusiastically engaged employee—who is fully committed to the organization's mission and looks forward to coming to work every day—is clearly going to be more productive than an angry, fearful worker or an automaton. The difference in productivity may only be 5 or 10%, but when global costs are taken into account, it is probably a great deal more.

This is not to say that discipline is unnecessary. The workplace clearly requires structure— requires rules and the exercise of authority. The need tends to arise most often in connection with employees' personal lives—sick time, vacation time, arrival and departure time and the like—and among employees performing the least complex tasks. Moreover, some employees routinely test limits, and they often require formal, sometimes inflexible, discipline. A prompt corrective response to misbehavior, whatever its motive, is indispensable as well to responsible employees, who would be aggrieved if bad behavior was tolerated or had no consequences. So discipline clearly needs to be in every manager's toolkit.

There is, however, a crucial distinction: the entrepreneur leads with the carrot and uses the stick only when absolutely necessary—and so creates for his employees the impression not only that they are responsible for the success of their department or organization but also that they are valued, supported and safe. The autocrat, by contrast, by using the stick first, creates anxiety, uncertainty, and insecurity, and conjures a hope that, by doing as asked, the employee may someday feel less anxious, uncertain and unsafe. It is not for no reason that autocracy is sometimes called by other names: dictatorship, tyranny, despotism, totalitarianism and arrogance are also used to describe a kind of behavior that our country, in other contexts, usually frowns upon, not only because it is unpleasant and amoral, but also because it is generally ineffective. There is little question about which workplace employees prefer. It is pretty clear as well that, though the siren song of uncomplicated autocracy still appeals to many in the boardroom and many executive leaders, the entrepreneurial workplace has an edge in optimizing productivity as well.

– 17 –

Character—1

So here is the first principle for hiring a manager: Hire an enthusiast, someone who encourages and empowers people, and who can help employees align their skills and capacities with the mission of your organization. Discipline has its uses, but it is important to keep in mind that productivity depends on the human instinct to create, to build, to excel. Few among us want to be told what to do, and fewer still want to be told how to do it (even if this is precisely what has to happen). Fortunately, there are many talented managers who can elicit effort by asking, supporting, demonstrating, and encouraging, who can, if you like, create miracles of productivity by treating people well. Those are the managers you will want to hire and support. Don't worry if you cannot identify such individuals yet. There is much more to come that should help. For now, we will turn to four other traits important for choosing suitable managers: first, two that tend to track closely with autocracy/entrepreneurship, and then two that associate somewhat more independently.

The Interchangeable Parts Paradigm

– 18 –

A Diverse Society

"It takes all kinds to make a world." We've heard it said. And, by the time we reach the workplace, most of us are pretty unique—we began with different parents or caretakers, had different interests and preferences, came from different cultures and backgrounds, have had different experiences, lived in different milieus in different parts of the world, had different friends, taken different training, developed different biases and expectations, had different traumas and losses, developed different beliefs—and, of course, have each of us, our own unique set of genes, sex, and skin color. That we live in a melting pot and so draw a wide variety of employees from what is still, despite the variety, a common culture is generally considered an asset. All these different folks coming together create a productive ferment—and this convergence of unique perspectives can elegantly solve difficult problems. Moreover, workplaces have become increasingly complex and finding someone appropriate for the various indispensable roles is facilitated by having a wide array of skilled workers among whom to choose. However, realizing these benefits depends upon management that can recognize and utilize the various skillsets and coordinate constructive interaction among them. As a rule, entrepreneurial managers embrace this healthy diversity, while autocratic managers are less enthusiastic, preferring to assign tasks randomly, without matching the task to the worker's skills.

Some autocrats are frankly disconcerted by diversity. Often they have chosen to live their private lives in like-minded monoculture enclaves and have little prior exposure to those with different backgrounds. Moreover, when they reach for a tool to accomplish a task, they want a familiar tool. They do not want to hear about that tool's quirks or provenance; they reject tools they did not ask for. It is still not uncommon, even in large, diverse twenty-first-century corporations, to find such managers exercising their prejudices. Though no manager can publicly admit any longer to such predispositions since they are illegal and perilous for careers, being white and male can be, even today, an asset for appreciation and promotion. They can also, without risk, choose the short over the tall, the thin over the fat, and the pretty over the plain. Diversity can, in other words, be managed by unequal treatment, sponsoring a small cultural or behavioral group to lead, receive rewards, and rule the roost.

More common is a species of willful blindness to diversity. By ignoring the differences between people, by treating them as if they were all identical, interchangeable parts, and using them for daily tasks accordingly, another kind of autocrat accomplishes an assembly line of the spirit, a tendency we can call leveling. Many managers are levelers, predisposed either to treat workers as if they all came from the same mold, thus literally achieving the expectations of the Equality Opportunity Act—the height or color or training or sex of any individual is irrelevant. All are equal when it comes to the assignment of tasks.

Many among us have found the treatment under law of a

corporation as an individual mystifying. It is, after all, demonstrably a complex, ramifying entity composed of hundreds, thousands, even hundreds of thousands. However, an autocratic leveler can tell you that a corporation has only one will, one leader, one head. Its workers, its managers, and the entire hierarchy of employees function as support for one individual, for they all operate as extensions of his nervous system, obey his commands, and move according to his will. An autocratic corporation is, in that sense, one large complex individual. Where the autocrat functions as the brain, the entrepreneur is more of a catalyst, working with a team of autonomous individuals toward optimal outcomes, which is why the idea of an entrepreneurial corporation as an individual can seem ludicrous.

There are even astute and adroit autocrats who are far more subtle in their approach to diversity; some even win awards for their diversity programs, though their appreciation remains a relatively superficial one. Such autocrats may have a politician's memory for the names of employees, and sometimes their wives and children, their hobbies, recent or upcoming travel, and the like. Using a physical or mental Rolodex to store traits and preferences, even to send cards to employees on their birthdays, can be an appealing and successful, if mechanical, way to acknowledge and motivate individuals. Such leaders will often make episodic social and motivational calls, and though, during such visits, they usually respond noncommittally to questions about institutional policy and direction, the visits can generate substantial goodwill. They rarely, however, take any deeper interest in their employees as people or in their work-related passions. Their engagement is with the minutiae of personality. They tend to summarize a life and its beliefs in a few words or a phrase. Often obsessed with what motivates each individual, they do not take an interest in, and rarely remember, their employees' special skills, ambitions, or beliefs, or the books they read or the ideas they may have for change and improvement. This is because even the enlightened autocrat gains and uses his knowledge principally for purposes of manipulation—to get his employees to do what he wants, not to help them do what they want. At its heart, the entire interaction is a condescension that acknowledges and then exploits the trivialities of diversity but does not make any meaningful use of it.

Acknowledging an employee's individuality can have a powerful impact. Even just recalling his name and circumstances can generate some gratitude, loyalty, and increased effort. Asking about an employee's hopes, dreams and ideas can have a broader effect and can be even more powerfully liberating. That is the province of the best entrepreneurial leaders, who will also visit each employee individually, but usually with a more willing ear and more open agenda than the best autocrat. The goal of the entrepreneur is to identify, discuss, and come to understand and value the dreams of her employees and, when possible, to help them to realize those dreams. It is often the first time anyone, outside friends or family, has ever asked about an employee's private beliefs or aspirations, and the discussions can be quite tentative at first and then galvanizing as an individual begins to talk about and reconsider his ideas in the reflection of another's attention and the light of reason. The desire to learn new skills, to take on new roles can become a passion; long-held beliefs can be replaced by new ones, and workers can gain new maturity and commitment. Frustrations and anger can grow or melt away. The experience can be transformative, though it can take time. Here is where the best managers can have perhaps their greatest impact on the health and satisfaction of employees and on the bottom line. It is about assigning two formerly incompatible employees from diverse backgrounds to jointly manage a project, but it is also about each employee finding a way to employ his enthusiasm, the things he is best at and enjoys doing, to build a better company. The manager helps each employee to make this attempt and helps him to find a suitable venue.

– 19 –

Consultancy, with a Focus on Engineering

At least three good new tools or tactics can also be repurposed, or diverted from their original intent, by autocratic leaders to provide them less invidious ways to moderate the impact of diversity. Their leveling can and does harness common business school practices for such a purpose: among them consultancy, cross-training and the culture of learning.

Autocrats often turn to consultants. Sometimes they are hired simply to serve as propaganda: to support an initiative the leader has decided to introduce, but suspects will be unpopular and so divert the displeasure to outside *experts*. Sometimes the autocrat is genuinely uncertain about the appropriate direction to take. In either case, an autocrat likes to bring in someone he can control, who can, whenever possible, provide a comprehensive and systematic solution. Where an entrepreneur will tend to consult his own staff, books and research, mentors, or colleagues informally and proceed more cautiously by trial and error, autocrats prefer a change that comes as a surprise and is impressive and dramatic.

Autocrats believe in greatness: that a handful of men and women in every generation are special, wise, expert, skilled, and marked out for leadership. The autocrats themselves are among the chosen, of course, but so also are the consultants they hire. If "no man is a prophet in his own home," choosing a consultant or consultant team with a formidable or trendy reputation can serve the purpose. Because they believe that once the proper direction is chosen, money will follow, they can choose more on the basis of the eloquence, authority and elegance of the consultants' delivery and their programmed solutions than on evidence of their success in comparable institutions and situations. Entrepreneurs recognize that the best approach is one that not only is proven but also captures the imagination of their workers.

Because consultants are invited by leaders and serve at their pleasure, successful ones quickly learn to tailor their reports to the biases of those who hire them. Engineers are just one brand of consultant, though they can be an especially useful one and are in vogue recently because they have specific relevant training; industrial engineers are, in fact, trained to address just the sort of issues we have been discussing. The earliest engineers were efficiency experts, who analyzed jobs by breaking them into their component parts and, where possible, defined the one optimal way, the one right way to complete each individual task, which everyone should follow. Their ultimate tool for measurement was usually the stopwatch, and the Holy Grail was speed: how can tasks be done most quickly? The assembly line was where they got their start, and it does lend itself best to their methodology. Changes they suggested in the early twentieth century clearly improved productivity, and many of the processes they illuminated, because they can be done best in only one way, are done today by machines or robots. However, many aspects of our workplace remain inefficient. A good workplace efficiency expert, now usually referred to as an engineer, can be invaluable, for example, in addressing flow, space, and the optimal use of the computer keyboard. Still, most tasks in the workplace do not yield only one best means of accomplishment. Different people approach them differently and fruitfully. Now, though, the successes of the efficiency expert can have a large psychological impact. Many administrative minds share the behaviorist fantasy that if we could only get all workers to do all tasks in precisely the same way, if, as in the movie *Metropolis*, rooms of people could move in unison, we could be infinitely more productive. It is not so, of course. Each suggested efficiency should be taken on its merits and introduced accordingly. It is important to keep in mind that the engineer representing employees on a spreadsheet, diagram or pie chart can be far removed from the living, breathing human doing tasks and her manipulations of what look like identical work units can consequently go astray. The best engineering results are generally obtained from engineers physically present in the workplace, working iteratively with managers and workers to fine-tune activities.

Other consultants are often more opinionated with less justification. Most suggest dramatic and thoroughgoing changes in behavior that constitute leveling. For example, everyone should meet before work in the morning to pledge one thing or another. Everyone should wear a particular uniform, complete various checklists to document tasks completed or use a set of scripts to interact with fellow workers or the public. It is hard to measure the impact of such interventions. Consultants benefit from what is called the Hawthorne effect, identified in the 1930s at the Hawthorne Works, a Western Electric factory near Chicago: simply focusing attention on an aspect of one's work and making any change, regardless of the nature of the change, can temporarily improve productivity.

I certainly hope that one prominent script actually improves productivity, because I find it a constant irritant. When floor-walkers or cashiers ask me, "*Did* you find everything OK?" I hold my tongue; they are required to use the script, and it would not be appropriate to trouble them with my clever response of the week. Still, the question has never led me to a further purchase or to discuss my ability to find items in their store; it has simply been an aversive episode near the end of every shopping experience for the past twenty-five years.

I have no doubt that consultants, and in particular engineering consultants, make valuable suggestions that improve productivity and that at least some of that contribution is due to leveling. However, I also believe that, before adopting any such recommendation, one should have to have good reason to believe that introducing it will be superior to the persistence of variety and superior to consulting your workers, your resident experts, on how to do their jobs best. Good reason is usually reliable and generalizable evidence that it has worked in a similar setting previously.

– 20 –

Cross Training

Cross training affords autocrats another opportunity to treat all employees as if they were functionally indistinguishable from one another; though used as it was originally intended, it can also be a valuable approach in appropriate settings. Training employees to do two unrelated jobs can save money, provide coverage, and give employees an opportunity to learn and apply new skills, and to add some variety to their workday. Training cashiers, for instance, to act as stocking clerks can be helpful or harmful, depending upon the circumstances. Let's posit, for the moment, that turnover and absences are common in both groups and that the jobs really do involve entirely different sets of skills. Cross training both departments would clearly provide the best coverage for absences. It would also offer employees a break from doing the same thing day after day and teach them new skills. Whether the manager is autocratic or entrepreneurial would not determine which approach to take. From the autocrat's perspective, the employees will be functioning as interchangeable parts either way (though they are more prone to cross train the entire department if they choose cross training). With the skillsets separated, he will have a set of identical clerks and a set of identical cashiers; with the skillsets merged, he will have two one size-fits-all clerks/cashiers, all, in theory equally capable. The entrepreneur is more likely to take the employees' concerns and desires into account, to begin by trying to ascertain what is causing the turnover. If the turnover is due to the sameness of each task, cross training may prove to be ideal. However, if most of the employees prefer one job or the other, asking for volunteers to cross train may be a better solution. Cross training five employees may be more sensible than cross training twenty-five. It is important to keep in mind as well that doing a job regularly reinforces skills. If large numbers of employees are crossing over infrequently, they may be damagingly inefficient in their crossover role.

Where there are two related sets of tasks and the need for coverage is frequent so that each skillset is reinforced by repeated use, where clerks and secretaries in the same department, for example, can learn each other's roles and cover one another during absences, cross training is an excellent resource. When the tasks are more diverse, however, and/or the need for coverage is less frequent, the value of cross training diminishes. And when cross training involves employees in tasks they dislike, it can decrease morale and effectiveness and do more harm than good. In that case, unless the intent is to give employees a break from a deadly routine and make a second role a part of their responsibilities (and the costs in training and efficiency are not too great), cross training one or two workers who volunteer is in practice generally more successful than cross training entire departments. It can also be preferable to simply have a part-time coverage pool—not to cross train all teachers, for example, to cover both high school and elementary school students, but to hire specialized substitute teachers to cover absences, one set for high and one set for elementary school students.

– 21 –

Culture of Learning

An allied concept is grandly called a culture of learning. Creating such a culture can be transformational: it can enrich employees' lives by helping them learn new skills, build confidence, learn new approaches to familiar tasks, understand others' perspectives; to grow, earn promotions, become more efficient and effective, and thus improve organizational productivity. One facet of this culture is formal teaching; and because good teaching can be time-consuming and take employees away from their work, there is an understandable tendency not only to hold employees accountable for what they learn, but also to make the learning, whenever possible, on-the-job training, or schedule it before work, during lunch, or grudgingly for a half-day on a complex subject. While useful new functions for a computer program may lend themselves comfortably to such a schedule, introducing the concept of teams may require a more comprehensive and leisurely approach.

Once again, where the line is drawn between voluntary and coercive tends to be crucial. Autocrats can and do use the culture of learning to expand the responsibilities of their workers. One widespread practice involves sending large groups of employees to time-limited training sessions and then expecting them all to have mastered the new skill and to incorporate it into their work. A secretarial pool might be sent, for example, to learn how to use complex spreadsheets to enter travel costs for an organization where travel is common and where the travel department has previously been responsible—and where many of the secretaries have never used a spreadsheet before. Workers sometimes call this "mission creep." You may recall that my sister-in-law (first vignette, page 1) left food technology because she received limited mandatory training in marketing, and it then became part of her job.

Of course, the pertinence, quality, and nature of the training matter a good deal as well. The incorporation of adult learning theory, enthusiasm, and an ability to connect with learners, a true mastery of a subject and clear communication of a small number of important lessons at a time, an opportunity for learners to ask questions and to, hands-on, apply what they have learned, all contribute to a successful program. Learning tends to be most effective when the employee is relaxed, wants to learn, has the time and the support for the program, and understands its need and value and how it can help her personally to do her job more effectively or efficiently.

Teaching employees what they spontaneously recognize they need in the course of their daily work, tailoring the training to the learning needs and learning styles of the individuals, saving classroom training for general principles and overviews are likely to have the largest impact and create a true lifelong culture of learning. An employee with computer skills, who can help others when they are stuck with a function of Excel, for example, who can stop by and give pointers, can talk at meetings about what's new in the new version or how to *pretty up* graphs, who can train new employees, creates value that more than justifies the freedom and time to provide the training. Ideally one discovers and encourages such education from within, organic connections that create a true culture of learning. This informal, individual, incremental, interactive education by someone who knows your work (and so what you need to know to make you more efficient and happier) tends to be far more effective than a separate education department. Moreover, when one recalls what folks take away from large group training sessions (7% of a typical lecture), the informal approach is at least as efficient as a separate education department with a separate culture and different goals. Employees in formal education settings often confront a set of inflexible lessons that don't take into account what each already knows or individual learning styles; that takes place in required classes one often has to register for in advance through a time-consuming, user-unfriendly computer program (to create a record of who took which courses when), scheduled at the teacher's convenience often at a distance from the workplace, with required post-tests and satisfaction forms to complete. What formal education there is should be, whenever possible, voluntary, quick and easy to access, and should help each employee to learn what she needs to learn to become more effective, confident, knowledgeable, competent, capable, and productive, and it should promote unique skills and capacities. It should not be undertaken to *demonstrate* that all employees have been trained in *infection control*, for example, so that the company can indicate such in its pro-motional literature, though employees have learned little or nothing useful.

It is preferable that a culture of learning not be about trying to pour the same set of principles, rules and approaches into the heads of all employees so that they come to see the same way, think the same things, act in the same manner; that is a coercive leveling fantasy. It should be about how to encourage and benefit from diversity, not about how to stifle it.

– 22 –
Character–2

And so you will probably want to hire someone who genuinely enjoys and values diversity and promotes or empowers syner-gies between different disciplines, departments, and cultures;

someone unrelenting about mission and goals but flexible about means; someone with the tolerance and resourcefulness to create a productive environment by using all the skills of each person optimally; someone who is likely to spend more time with her employees, encouraging, watching, explaining, suggesting (and yes also insisting), learning, teaching, sharing, building than on the computer with spreadsheets, e-mail, and action plans. On a spreadsheet, it is far too easy to turn an electrician into a plumber and to forget that this particular electrician had two years of engineering, is left-handed, loves tight spaces, and has a reputation for throwing a great party.

– 23 –

Mythical Leaders

Startup companies are run by impresarios. Those who make good have come to be seen as models for what successful leaders should be. Of course, our mental portrait of such successful leaders gets drawn on the basis of what they are like after they have achieved their success and what works for startups may not work for established companies. Still, the general popular impression is of an autocrat: a forceful extrovert, egotistical and larger than life, ambitious, greedy, and ready to sell the company and move on to new personal career challenges or, if she stays, build a monument to herself in corporate headquarters, amass art collections, and corporate history. Such caricatural impresarios rule their companies with an iron hand. This is clearly a reductive and imperfect picture of successful real life financiers. (We will consider them further when we look for models of who to hire.) And it is the portrait of someone who will almost certainly fail as a leader of an established corporation. But, just as the bias toward hiring disciplinarians has hampered workplace productivity, so too has the hiring of self-interested careerist superstars resulted in unsatisfactory performance.

– 24 –

Good to Great

Many persons have a wrong idea of what constitutes true
happiness. It is not attained through self-gratification but through
fidelity to a worthy purpose.
—Helen Keller

For *Good to Great*, Jim Collins put together a team that re-
searched companies that had once been average performers
and then had cumulative stock market returns three or more
times the average for their industry yearly for fifteen years or
more, a suitable surrogate measure of productivity. He discovered that all eleven outperforming companies (and very few of
their competitors) had what he called level five leaders.

As Collins puts it, "Level 5 leaders channel their ego needs
away from themselves and into the larger goal of building a
great company. It's not that level five leaders have no ego or
self-interest. Indeed, they are incredibly ambitious—*but their
ambition is first and foremost for the institution, not themselves.*" Level five leaders are "quiet, reserved, self-effacing,
even shy," they are "modest and willful, humble and fearless...
more plow horse than show horse." They are not larger-than-
life extrovert celebrities focused on their own careers and fu-
tures, full of talk and bluster about what they can accomplish;
they are quiet, intense, committed, often introverts; and they
take responsibility for failures and attribute successes to good
luck and their teams.

Being an entrepreneur does not mean giving up the reins
of governance; it means separating off the ego and functioning not as a hero but as an agent. Though she may look like a
hero to her direct reports as she fights for their resources, or

feel like one herself when working for an autocratic regime and having to do battle for every inch of progress against resistance, in fact, the entrepreneurial leader is dispassionate about the work's meaning for herself and her renown and passionate about its meaning for everyone else—for employees, coworkers, customers, shareholders, and administrators. Entrepreneurial leaders are altruists—not by design but by conviction. And yet they are particular and rigorous altruists. They only accept the best outcomes for everyone. This can, for example, make them tough negotiators when common interests do not prevail in initial talks with unions, allies, or competitors.

Perhaps because the book is only twenty years old, perhaps because it has only sold a few million copies, perhaps because it challenges entrenched prejudices and is counterintuitive, its findings seem to have had little impact on hiring, at least at the organizations where I, my family, friends, and acquaintances work, and at the ones in the news. J.C. Penney's has been just the most recent and rapidly evolving example of choosing a celebrity leader as a form of public institutional suicide. Here, in *Good to Great*, though, is hard evidence that entrepreneurial management is economically superior to autocratic.

– 25 –

Loyalty

Although all managers are partial to appreciative, supportive employees, autocrats tend to require them and so to be obsessed with loyalty. They usually identify lieutenants early on, people they can trust to defend all their plans, programs, and propaganda without questioning them, and to speak as they would—to, as the cliché has it, cover their backs. Most autocrats find it hard to tolerate opinions at variance with their own. They prefer a quiet workplace *where you can hear a pin drop*, with everyone in it working *like clockwork* according to principles they, the autocrats, have defined. Otherwise they *can't hear themselves think* and things are likely to *spin out of control*. Structured and organized behavior makes it easier to identify when someone is behaving badly and get him back in line. Presenting another approach, trying out new ideas, and disagreeing are often viewed as insubordination and can be disproportionately punished, though if they overhear a particularly good idea they may well adopt it for their own without attribution. They want to *make sure* that they are protected, and that there is no question about who is boss and who gets credit for success.

To an entrepreneurial manager, the loyalty autocrats value is a narrow commodity and as often harms as helps them. Whether or not she has them, she keeps her employee preferences to herself. She knows that nearly everyone is sensitive on the subject of their own value and that good ideas can come from anyone. She also knows that workers who have tried out new ideas or contradicted her have often helped and protected her and that constructive conflict is more often productive than unreflective acquiescence. She is not seeking protection or credit, just greater productivity and a more effective pursuit of the mission. To achieve them, she prefers a cheerful and interactive workplace, humming with energy, a productive ferment, knowing that networking leads to new ideas and employees thrive where they can freely express themselves. Such a manager actually finds it easier to identify and manage laziness, exploitation, ineffectiveness, or subversion in a complex environment, particularly when employees feel safe to express themselves, than in a subdued and chastened workplace. In time, self-regulation becomes the rule, and, in general, in mature entrepreneurial workplaces, employees hold themselves and their coworkers to higher standards than autocratic managers would dare to hope for, much less mandate. A workplace built on trust and verification is invariably more productive than one built on rules—fruitlessly, in many contemporary workplaces, there seems to be nearly one *overseer* for every frontline worker, to tell that worker what to do and how to do it and to make sure it gets done in the manner prescribed.

– 26 –

Success Defined

Autocrats like explicit contracts. Whenever possible, they will negotiate with their bosses to define success as concretely and narrowly as possible—an increase in share price, an improvement in market share, an increase in the variety of products, the volume of each product fabricated, units sold, the acquisition of other companies. Meeting these goals, regardless of what else may happen on their watch, means career advancement: bonuses, salary increases, generous evaluations, promotions, and greater power. Bosses can feel they have more control over goals and a better idea of what they are paying for.

But entrepreneurial leaders know in their bones that narrowing the focus will limit success. Their responsibility is to struggle creatively every day, using all the resources at their disposal, to advance every aspect of the mission, to decrease cost, increase quality, build greater capacity, satisfy all their constituencies, and improve the society at large. Only in this way will the greatest increases possible in share price, market share, and quality measures be achieved, not only this year but for the next fifty years—while the happy and prosperous employees will enrich the lives of their children who may one day also work for the firm. This can mean obsessive thinking and rethinking about processes, which can mean thinking outside the box, which can render contracts and action plans meaningless: because so much changes, midyear goals are often markedly different from those set at the start. To be successful, she creates teams that are lean and mean and able to turn on a dime right alongside those built for the long haul. Not only is there no time or opportunity in the midst of this effort, but they have no interest in promoting themselves. They are too busy giving away credit to others, helping their employees to their own bonuses, promotions, career development, and building value for the corporation as a whole. It is not surprising that it is hard to identify model servant leaders. They are, as a rule, invisible, not famous.

– 27 –

Success Achieved

To be so unappreciated is undoubtedly sad for Blumfeld, but there is no remedy, for he cannot very well compel Ottomar to spend let us say a whole month on end in Blumfeld's department in order to study the great variety of work being accomplished there, to apply his own allegedly better methods, and to let himself be convinced of Blumfeld's soundness by the collapse of the department which would be the inevitable result.
—Franz Kafka, "Blumfeld, an Elderly Bachelor"

Though some, as noted earlier, will seek advice from mentors, superiors or formal consultants, many career builders starting out in a new position will move rapidly and, it can seem, haphazardly to make their mark. Rather than devoting an initial interval to learning about the culture, strengths and challenges, skills and ambitions of the institution from its leaders and workers, they may start to make changes, pretty much from day one. They may introduce an approach that has been suggested or imposed by their superior; one that worked for them in a previous workplace; one that they were taught in school; one that is trendy or feels comfortable; a clever approach that has never been tested; or one that seems to have no immediate downside—what might be called window-dressing. The goal in each case is to create an impression of progress that can be used in support of applications for better jobs for higher pay in a year or two. They may, for example, *downsize* to give an impression of fiscal responsibility, which may involve closing a productive unit or, by removing vital employees or funds, decrease a department's ability to prosper. Or they can pursue goals that give the impression of progress but are hard to measure, like modernization, reorganization or client-centeredness. The best of these initiatives are grandiose: "*Our* new supplement will eliminate obesity over the next three years;" or "with our genetically modified corn, we will put an end to hunger world-wide;" while the worst set no goals at all, introducing back-to-basics programs or defining everyday business as their vision. They take responsibility for any hint of success and blame any failures on the culture, other employees, the state of the economy, or their line of business.

What is common to all these scenarios is that they represent one person's imposed and inflexible initiative, only coincidentally connected to the mission. There is almost always substantial internal disagreement, initially expressed, then suppressed. The disagreement, unaddressed, turns to disappointment, anger, and frustration. And then, in a year or two, the leader moves on to greener pastures, and it is time for a new superstar.

Level five managers, in contrast, are, except in emergencies, patient and methodical; they introduce new initiatives after a period of intensive inquiry and discussion and stay until they have put their businesses on a sound trajectory. They address the basic business, its everyday operations and its expansion into new markets, develop related and new opportunities, acquisitions, and lines of business, build happy and prosperous workplaces, and assure succession before moving or retiring. They accept adversity as a challenge but do not contribute to it. They involve their leaders and workers, consider their advice and suggestions, and give credit to those with good ideas, often telling stories about how a clerk suggested one of the most important innovations the company had made or how a team came up with a plan that fixed a problem that had haunted the company for years.

Inspiration of Respect, Trust, and Confidence (RTC)

– 28 –

Context

Although the workplace provides them with dictatorial power, the best leaders feel themselves constrained by many forces, in particular by the force of opinion. Inspiring a positive opinion in those they manage, work beside, and work for is not an easy task since each group has rather different expectations. Some autocratic managers choose to solve this problem by opting out. They please their bosses but engage only fitfully and apathetically in the other fundamental relationships. Such a strategy, however, though it is not only viable but actually quite commonly utilized, never yields an optimal result. Nor is it consistent with the entrepreneurial workplace we identified earlier as indispensable to productivity. A fully successful manager will inspire respect, trust, and confidence in everyone he interacts with, but particularly in those he manages.

Neither autocrats nor entrepreneurs have a lock on stirring RTC. Autocrats benefit from hierarchy, publicity, ceremony, celebrity, and symbolism—they often become widely respected leaders, particularly when they are successful, personable, stylish, and reasonably fair. It usually takes far more effort for an entrepreneur to achieve similar success. In particular, employees who have been used to autocracy can be suspicious of and take a long time to trust a new leader, may take advantage of him, and may even have contempt for him at first for being soft. However, once there has been sufficient time for observation and familiarity, entrepreneurial leaders can end up inspiring not just RTC but veneration and affection.

– 29 –

Expertise

Employees, professional employees in particular, prefer someone with experience in the work he will be managing, if possible with long and distinguished experience, and ideally with some special insight into the work. That instinct is a good one. Selecting as manager someone from another discipline, or even an unseasoned individual trained in the field she will manage, frequently proves problematic. Nurses want to be managed by an experienced nurse, salespeople by salespeople, and engineers by engineers. As one moves higher in the organization, it generally remains best to choose someone with experience in the fields that are central to the organization's success, programmers for computer companies, and someone with clinical experience for health care institutions. And it is best when they loved that work and didn't become managers to escape it or, worse, to get revenge on others who did it better. Entrepreneurial leaders rarely have an interest in managing in a field in which they have no experience. However, since their commitment is to their careers and not to any given mission, autocrats are usually willing to take on any increase in responsibility offered. Unfortunately, they usually have less insight into their own suitability for any given task than entrepreneurs—they get less unbiased feedback, and they tend to feel more confident than their circumstances, whatever they may be, warrant.

At least at a subliminal level, we are all aware that even the best schoolroom education never completely prepares a new graduate for the job he will do in the workplace. In fact, training, even when one takes internships and practical rotations into account, can create many misconceptions and inefficiencies. Orientations, formal on-the-job training with educators and coworkers, informal training (in the short cuts, lay theories, and lore of the workplace), and continuing education help us to transform an inefficient, often clueless rookie into a seasoned, highly productive worker. (This long, costly development, along with the cost of recruitment and the formation and adjustment of relationships, is what makes retention, most often possible, preferable.) The best leaders have not only gone through this transformation and then helped others through it—they have also been critical thinkers from the start and so have continued to question and read about their discipline until their personal strategies are among the most efficient in at least a few practical workplace arenas. Moreover, they can *bottle* and generalize their discoveries—put them into words and teach others how to be more efficient and successful, which is the crux of special insights. Such special insights, because they go to the heart of what works best to accomplish each task, tend to be cost-saving and/or productivity generating, and they tend to fly below the radar, often because the academic discipline (and the efficiency experts) have overlooked their importance or misinterpreted it, often because neither the academics nor the efficiency experts have practical experience in the discipline. Often, therefore, the best candidates for leadership will also be excellent idiosyncratic teachers. That can be another way to recognize them: they often have taught, more often in some venue of practical experience rather than in the classroom, and they are often better liked by the students than by the faculty. They are often nominated for teaching awards but rarely win them.

– 30 –

Experience

Along with critical thinking and experience in one's field, training and experience in other disciplines can lay the groundwork for valuable perspectives, exchanges, and insights. A Human Resources manager with an MBA, of course, but also one with a Master's Degree in Psychology, or even Art History or training as a master chef, will, in general, be preferable to a candidate without, to foster both RTC and productivity. Ideas do tend to cross-pollinate, and two or three important insights effectively exploited can be the difference between an adequate and an outstanding performance over a decade's tenure in a department. Because autocrats recognize the importance of CVs to the careers they are determined to build, their CVs are nearly always complete, pertinent, and easy to understand. Entrepreneurs, on the other hand, rarely plan to become managers, and so their backgrounds may often appear unplanned. Pertinent experience may not even be included in their resumes and may need rooting out.

There is, in addition, a widespread misconception about education as well. Formal education in any discipline is, as a rule, valued more highly than experience in that same discipline, although experience is almost certainly more valuable than formal education. So, for example, a manager with an

MBA will be courted more avidly and valued and paid more highly than someone who owned, operated and sold a donut shop, even though the practical real-world experience will almost always provide better training than the academic classroom courses. Accepted wisdom is often wrong, while the *school of hard knocks* is an implacable taskmaster, but always right. A writer's workshop, a junior year abroad, a stint on a college soccer team, presidency of the local Four-H club, a job as a radio announcer, volunteer work as a librarian or political aide, cooking, gardening—all should be appreciated and carefully considered. Each provides opportunities to learn valuable skills and lessons that may cross-pollinate in your workplace and help to avoid errors and choose fruitful paths to productivity.

– 31 –

Performance

Respect, trust, and confidence must all be earned. They may be lent for a honeymoon period when a new manager first arrives—coworkers at all levels not only hope a new leader will succeed; they actively want her to; but each also has a yardstick against which he measures her. So the honeymoon period may not last all that long unless some of the hopes are fulfilled. A new entrepreneurial manager needs to quickly establish that she can address the needs and expectations of all three groups (and those outside the organization when they are part of her ambit). An autocrat, of course, need not please anyone but herself, since her goal is, in general, either to disappoint or redefine expectations or, whenever possible, to substitute her own yardstick in the minds of all the others.

Because they are usually the most exposed and fragile and the least patient, and their opinions are the hardest to recover once lost, a new leader is wise to start by meeting or exceeding the expectations of her subordinates, especially their natural leaders and opinion makers. They are the folks she has to lead, motivate and deliver in order to accomplish the tasks that will allow the organization to prosper—and, as noted above, this needs to occur relatively quickly. So, if you are doing the hiring, especially of an entrepreneur, it is best not to make what is a very common mistake. You will probably want to withhold judgment early on. You have done the due diligence of choosing the best possible person. Do not make her prove her value, her skills, and particularly her loyalty in the first few weeks. Observe, of course, discuss if necessary, and yes, intervene if she is going completely off the rails, but allow her broad latitude to establish credibility with her workers from the start. If necessary, play good cop, bad cop, and let her be the good cop. You will reap great benefits if your workers respect, trust, and have confidence in the new leader you have hired. It will also give them more RTC for you. So go all out with introductions and support, but let the new leader be seen to operate independently to represent the needs of her constituency. Trust her to understand what her workers need and want and even which things are safe and appropriate to grant or change and where to hold the line. It makes sense to meet regularly, to ask in advance what your new leader is considering and why, to be available when help or guidance is requested, and to make suggestions. But if you do not trust her judgment, if you try to impose your will, ask for written action plans or a timetable in advance, you may inadvertently box in or cripple your new leader and impair her reception in this crucial period.

– 32 –

Expectations

Though they will accept structure, consistency, and direction, and most will give their RTC to any leader who provides a predictable workplace, what employees want most from a supervisor are understanding, appreciation, and help; most are not looking for special treatment, just fair and equitable treatment. So the entrepreneurial first step in meeting their expectations is to ask their opinion. There may be crises or initiatives that require immediate attention; employees may be too numerous or too widely spread geographically for immediate face-to-face interactions. Still, it is best to find a way to request input and suggestions, if not from all, from as many of one's employees as can be managed as early on as possible, and that requires some form of reaching out. It should, at a minimum, even for autocrats, involve visiting each direct report where he or she works to get a preliminary orientation to their working environment, their resources and frustrations, and their ideas about the organization's challenges and opportunities—what do they think should be the next steps and the long term plans? It is preferable that such discussions not be pro forma, an agenda already determined and input requested and ignored when it does not agree with *the plan*; they should be true fact-finding visits to help determine what will be done. Of course, this helps to determine what kind of person to hire as a leader—someone who respects others individually, recognizes that one never knows where the next important idea will come from, believes that his employees are the resident experts about the workplace that they spend half their lives in, and can inspire them to share that expertise.

– 33 –

Fairness, Transparency, Recognition

The same principle—that everyone should be heard, that no decision should be taken without hearing all sides of an argument should apply in general. This requires ongoing outreach for opinion; along with a genuinely open door and regular meetings with ample opportunity for bottom-up as well as top-down discussion. Ideas and options, even when presented in anger, in opposition, or as grudges, should be encouraged and acted on appropriately. Creating a safe environment for such presentations and for all employees to make them requires creating a culture of civility, openness, and respect. (The anger, opposition and grudges have to be resolved, but, though in the entrepreneurial workplace that can often take a while, they do have to be expressed in order to be recognized and addressed, or if necessary extirpated.) In order to instill civility and respect, though, a new leader must demonstrate both for all employees, even as she demonstrates intolerance for incivility and disrespect and defines acceptable behavior. Such a leader must show interest, be accessible, transparent and fair, set expectations, and hold everyone equally accountable to meet them. She must understand, appreciate, and take to heart the obstructions that her employees encounter in their daily work, and find ways to reduce or eliminate them. And she must find a way to express her appreciation of her employees' efforts, a way that they feel recognizes what they have done. A simple "thank you" can often suffice; but special assignments, benefits, training, prizes, bonuses or raises used judiciously, and dependent on resources and organizational culture, can also be constructive. As a result, we are looking for servant leaders, individuals who gather information, make the workplace comfortable, equitable, and attractive, and identify and fix problems so that employees can operate at peak efficiency, in part because they don't waste many hours every week complaining to one another about their frustrations with obstructions and with their management.

– 34 –

Data

Though it is invaluable to have experience and good instincts, to have an intuitive sense of what will work, experience compels the best leaders to base their decisions and initiatives not only on intuitions but also on evidence to support or contradict those intuitions. They have to be willing to take risks, but each risk should be based upon a reasonable probability of success. As already noted, the views and experiences of employees are one form of evidence. The balance sheet is another. Customer satisfaction, the measurements of efficiency experts, and surrogate measures of success in the various areas of service and production are all useful. The best leaders, however, find new ways of looking at the workplace and introduce new, meaningful measures. They keep abreast of the study literature in their field, which defines scientifically what works and what does not. Received opinions, review articles, impressions, and one or two bottom-line outcome measures are not sufficient to excel. A leader must have in-depth knowledge of what works and what does not, and must be a master of data; must be certain it is accurate and follow its trends to understand as many pertinent aspects of work and production as possible to achieve the best outcomes. Being right and being successful are certainly vigorous wellsprings of RTC.

– 35 –

Cooperation

To gather this information, to hire new employees, discipline, discharge or find more appropriate places for those he inherits, to remove the obstructions to production that employees and the data identify, a leader needs help from other departments, in particular from human resources, information technology, quality, and buildings and maintenance. Therefore new managers will nearly always need to form effective relationships with the leaders of these other departments or their deputies or representatives, so that they can present and discuss needs and concerns, priorities, and areas of conflict and understand the needs and challenges of these departments. Cooperation to achieve common goals, ideally the goals of the organization's mission, makes the best common ground. Inspiring the respect, trust, and confidence of his fellow managers is a step on this path as well—and that requires consistency, sharing knowledge and information, keeping one's word, and making sure one's own department follows through on its responsibilities. It is preferable if the competition for resources, power, importance and the preferment of their boss do not become the motive forces behind these interactions (though managers must hold their ground and achieve the best possible outcomes, whatever the circumstances).

Communication Skills

– 36 –
Form of Address

Earning confidence, trust, and respect involves more than just background experience, knowledge, attitude, understanding and vision; one must also communicate how they matter clearly and well. What a leader says and when, where and how, help to define her in the minds and hearts of everyone she meets. Making the right choices—when to write and when to speak, at what point in any situation or negotiation; who to speak to—small groups or individuals, just one discipline, an entire department or multiple departments—where—offsite, in an auditorium, a conference room, by telephone, in her own office, where they work—depends on the wisdom and experience of a leader and on her skills: to strategize, to write, and to speak. Since many books have been fruitfully written about office communications, in this section we will focus on only a few pertinent facets of writing and speaking. Communications should be accurate and clear, concise and, at best, encouraging, and should often lift one's spirits because they are expressed so well and say so much. At least some, even during the stress and routine of application, should come as a welcome surprise.

Neither party has a monopoly on communication, either. Autocrats can be masterful public speakers; entrepreneurs can write warm, flawless prose; either can be a clumsy speaker, standoffish, tongue-tied, or confusing. However, whether adept or inept, their communications can, at least in some important respects, be in the service of divergent goals. We will look together now at a few key aspects of communication which may help us to choose productive managers.

– 37 –
The Relative Value of Truth

Perhaps the most important distinction between one leader and another in this arena is what they choose to say and not just how they say it. Entrepreneurs believe that at the base of all inspiring communication is conviction, truth, *telling it like it is*, and not using words as curtains to hide behind. Jargon, cliché and bland generalities may serve politicians who are trying to be all things to all people. We are all bombarded daily by newspeak and the blandishments, allurements, and outright lies of agents, advertisers, and fellow citizens who want us to believe in, buy from, invest in, help, or support them. Some remain easy to manipulate, but most of us become cynical. Nearly all recognize genuine truth when they hear it—and they desperately want to hear it in the work place but rarely do. They find that their bosses greet them and speak to them in the same self-interested way that the journalists and salespeople do, lie to them and try to manipulate them. When one tells them not what they want to hear but what is true, puts their needs, their frustrations, their aspirations, their situation into words that ring true, it is a galvanizing force.

But, for good reason, autocrats do not agree. They recognize that critical thinking is in short supply and that spin and propaganda can be extremely effective. So that, though when they are communicating a new policy, their vision for the future, an assignment, a reprimand—when they are defending a choice, negotiating a new contract, praising a subordinate's success, or telling a story about a trip to China, they may be speaking as openly, clearly and honestly as any entrepreneur, they can in every case be inventing at least some of their content out of whole cloth for any of a large variety of reasons. Manipulating truth is more often effective than entrepreneurs like to believe. Most employees give leaders the benefit of the doubt; when they recognize they cannot trust all the statements that are made by their leaders, they usually accept that some things cannot be shared; and, in such an environment, knowledge of the truth becomes a scarce commodity to be desired and pursued as actively as salary or benefits.

Still, I would argue that entrepreneurs are more right than autocrats when the monitors are employee health and productivity. Truth is healthier, more efficient, and more productive. Spin and propaganda can be surprisingly effective, but they are distorted, flawed and risky in ways that become increasingly evident over time. Therefore, I maintain that telling as much truth as possible, as much of the time as possible, is a valuable but surprisingly rare commodity, and one that we should look for and cherish in an entrepreneurial leader.

– 38 –

Even at a Distance

It is rarely cost-effective and not always practical in large in-stitutions to meet face-to-face with those with whom we need to communicate. Communication at a distance, by video, tele-phone, telephone conference, or e-mail, is often understand-ably disparaged, but it can be extremely effective in many situations. E-mail is efficient for the communication of most emotion-free information: announcements, invitations, re-minders about task deadlines and upcoming meetings; news, summaries of ideas or events, sharing of agendas. Calendars of events and libraries of minutes, policies, and technical sup-port are also best stored and shared electronically, by e-mail, on sharepoints, and at web sites.

Face-to-face meetings *are* the gold standard for controver-sial, emotion-laden or interactive issues, where participation, group dynamics, cross-fertilization, spontaneity, and nonver-bal communication make important contributions. However, when in-person meetings are not practical or are simply not possible, much can still be accomplished. I myself, a few years ago, was assigned to chair a committee of fourteen members scattered across the country. Of course, I would have preferred at least one face-to-face meeting early on, but we were never provided with the resources to meet in person. And, despite the challenges, over a three-year period, we did manage to develop a national report that met with general acclaim for its richness and usefulness, entirely by e-mail, sharepoint, and over the telephone.

So in choosing leaders, it is best to hire those who excel in both written and verbal communication. In writing friendly discursive notes, or e-mails, formal policy statements, compelling information summaries, and cool-headed appropriate responses (by the appropriate means) to provocative, inappropriate, or disheartening ones are all essential. Effective public speaking before small and large groups is quite a different skill from running a meeting. Whether the goal is to present information, brainstorm, build consensus, address a crisis or rebellion, discuss or explain tragedy, a failure, a loss, or a need, to ask for help that will require time, effort, or sacrifice, running a meeting, because it is interactive, it is a bigger challenge and a different skill. And it is again another to meet with employees individually, simply to say hello and interact, to gather information, provide positive feedback, review an evaluation, or present formal discipline. The leader who creates a positive response in the majority of his audience in every one of these circumstances is the best prospect. How can you tell? It may not be easy, but it is usually not sufficient to trust your own instincts at the interview. Feedback from interviewers at all levels, in particular those who will be working closely with the new hire, review of application communications, any preserved video or published materials, and request for sample writings may all be helpful.

– 39 –

Applied to Hiring

Probably the single most important thing a leader does is to hire, to choose the most suitable candidate for each position. Of course, in a global sense, this book addresses how to select a leader, and because leaders also select leaders, the principles should be the same. Here, however, our focus is on one important aspect of hiring, often considered the province of human resources: how to optimize the likelihood that the candidate we choose will come. From the content, layout, and placement of the advertising to the people involved in and character of the contacts, the speed of processing, arrangement of interviews, response to questions, nature of interview, opportunity for social interaction, relationship formed with the candidate, data gathered efficiently from all who meet the applicant and put into useful form, and persistence when a candidate is considering alternatives, a manager can have an outsized impact on whether the best prospects join your firm. You will certainly want to hire someone good at hiring.

It is common, and can be quite useful, to request that candidates provide references from professional associates. In reviewing these recommendations, however, the highest value is generally placed on the assessments provided by the candidates' managers, and that may not be appropriate. It is true that if you are going to manage someone yourself; it is reassuring to hear that a prior boss has approved of the candidate's performance. Nonetheless, evaluations by a candidate's subordinates or colleagues are likely to provide greater insight into the candidate's approach to, and success with, management than those of her superiors. If you want to know whether a candidate is autocratic or entrepreneurial, how much, and in what way, someone who was at the receiving end is in the best position to comment. Consequently, it may be well to specify that you would like at least two references from direct reports among the references a candidate supplies.

Though impartiality is often promoted as desirable, even as a gold standard of interviewing, one form of encouragement that is often effective, in my experience, is to let the best candidates know how well you think of them and how much you would like them to come to work with you. Use of this approach does require judgment, since not everyone responds well to positive feedback. Just as most employees respond to positive evaluations by increasing their effort, while some can only be motivated by the communication of reservations, so while most candidates will be more likely to accept a job when praised, some may require a measure of detachment as motivation. Still, in general, the in-person interview provides an opportunity to begin the formation of a warm and positive working relationship with a candidate. The promise of some genuine recognition of the individuality of a candidate (and her family when appropriate) can have an extremely positive impact; a dinner out during the visit can be decisive. This can be the beginning of a relationship that can continue for years, with regular strategic visits throughout the career of the new hire. The goal is something between a true friendship (such a relationship being a complication few leaders can, or should try to, successfully negotiate) and a superficial recognition such as we have seen autocrats often cultivate. It should extend to more than just the weather, vacations, and the family, and involve professional and career goals, philosophy of life, ambitions, hobbies, and pastimes.

– 40 –

Applied to Listening

Communication is a two-way street. The manager, whether motivating, defining, directing, reporting, summarizing, challenging, or provoking is most often the opening writer or speaker, the initiator of interactions and conversations. Yet, even while speaking to large groups from a prepared text, he will scan his audience for verbal and nonverbal clues about their perception, about his reception, and he will adjust his tone and even his content accordingly. In less formal environments, the best communicators often proceed to say the least.

They are comfortable with silence; they will perform introductions and may introduce the purpose of an interaction, and set others at ease, but then will often allow those others to launch the interaction, choose its initial direction and introduce a tone, which leaders can then modify as appropriate. They smile, nod, make eye contact, focus, mirror, ask questions, repeat comments or paraphrase, sprinkle compliments, and summarize.

As noted earlier, it is also appropriate to ask for and to utilize the opinions, proposals and ideas of employees. That involves not only outreach, the open door, hearing both sides of an argument, creating safety, thanking volunteers for their input, and holding regular meetings; it also involves being out and about and asking formal and informal questions. Input can be enhanced by having a part of a regular meeting devoted to answering employee questions, addressing rumors and the like. But perhaps the most galvanizing and meaningful approach to creating a truly two-sided conversation is for a leader to ask for input about his/her performance. This can be, and often is, done informally, and it is occasionally done as part of a "360;" this customarily involves a leader in training requesting input from a selection of coworkers according to a formal training program protocol. However, it is rarely a part of formal annual evaluations in a meaningful way. An organization where each employee evaluates her/his supervisor each year with a reasonably comprehensive instrument will not only have one of the best mechanisms for feedback and input from employees, but will also be a giant step along the way to well-informed and appropriately humble servant leaders. The best leaders will welcome such input; and they will introduce it into their departments if it does not exist.

What Employers Need to Know: Hiring from Above

– 41 –

The Need for an Instrument

Since employees seem often to be disgruntled and leaders prefer the reputation and recognition of being *employers of choice* over the ignominy of employee dissatisfaction, many companies have, over the years, administered a wide variety of surveys and hired researchers to try to understand their workers' concerns; in addition, journalists have not infrequently conducted surveys and interviews to sample employees' opinions about their bosses and their work. When employees who feel safe enough to express their true concerns are asked about their bosses, they say many things that we would expect from our discussion about what makes a good boss. Less than half of them think they have a good boss, which, of course, means that almost half of them do. They complain about arrogance, inflexibility, narcissism, greed, micromanagement, risk-aversion, disinterest, unavailability, dissembling, inconsistency, uncertainty, confusion, deceit, laziness, indecision, impulsivity, negativity, dishonesty, manipulation, fabrication, nastiness, incompetence.

They complain of an inability to set direction; an unwillingness to listen; of hiring, promoting, and giving raises for loyalty rather than skill; of taking credit for the work of others and giving none to those deserving; of giving credit only to favorites. They deplore the predisposition to shoot the messenger; an unwillingness to pitch in and help out: to work at the front desk, to challenge underperforming employees, to use political capital to help remove obstructions; a preference for dealing with crises rather than preventing them, for taking a hard line on rules, policies and precedents to the exclusion of improvement, creativity, and innovation; for the creation of an atmosphere of competition, uncertainty, anger, and fear, of cliques, rumors, sarcasm, and complaint.

Such a list can afford considerable insight into the challenges employees feel they face. It might even be expanded to create a more comprehensive picture of what can go wrong in a workplace. But it delivers a composite picture that provides little direction for someone trying to choose a suitable leader. Some bad managers are lazy, and some are energetic. Some are risk-averse, and some always operate on the edge. Some religiously follow rules, and others create their own. Some provide too little discipline, some too much, and some just the right amount but to the wrong people or at the wrong time or too privately or too publicly. Because it was clear to me that it would be extraordinarily useful to have a theory that could simplify this embarrassment of riches and help act as a guide in choosing a manager who can address or forestall nearly all these concerns, we have been considering the autocratic/ entrepreneurial divide and the four subsidiary domains.

I have not specifically addressed, for example, storytelling, negotiation, or emotional intelligence in my discussion of the model, though they can all be valuable skills. I have not specifically addressed bullying or amorality either. For, as I have tried to provide some clarity in this untidy world, they have not seemed to be fundamental to choosing leaders, and they are hard to evaluate. That being said, to reinforce our model, let's briefly summarize what, I have suggested, does matter most.

– 42 –

The Instrument, Its Characteristics and Its Provisional Nature

a.

Each of the five central issues we have discussed, listed here in what I think is the order of their importance, can be viewed as a continuum between two poles:

1. Autocratic ———————— Entrepreneurial

2. Treats employees as ———— Treats employees as separate
interchangeable parts   individuals

3. Focuses on career ———— Focuses on mission

4. Inspires little trust, ———— Inspires full trust, respect, and
respect, or confidence   confidence

5. Communicates sub-obtimally — Communicates well

Of course, we *could* simplify each continuum or break them down further. Communication could, for example, be divided into component parts—communicates poorly or well in writing, in speech, at large face-to-face group meetings, and during phone calls with subordinates. Or communication could be subsumed into number 4, reducing our guide to only four central continua since one inspires trust, respect, and confidence by communicating well after all. We could also make the model more complicated: as noted above, other continua could be added or substituted; or some of the continua be turned into triangles or quadrangles by adding poles—we could, for example, add Rational and/or Supportive management to Autocratic and Entrepreneurial.

I mention these considerations in order to acknowledge

that this construct can at this time be, like any new decision-making tool, only a proposal, however persuasive, which will need more testing than my observation and experience and that of a few associates have so far provided. However, it does reflect what I believe is a profound and determinative set of insights into a field that has been neglected. As a guide to hiring managers, I submit that this is the most practical and useful structure you will find anywhere.

b.

If each applicant were equally likely to fall anywhere along each scale, an infinite number of different leadership candidates would be possible. You could, for example, choose to hire an altruistic autocrat, who treats employees as individuals, inspires confidence, and communicates well, a prince among autocrats. Within the sober confines of this real world, however, you are unlikely ever to find one—for while most autocrats communicate well and many inspire respect and a significant degree of confidence in large numbers of employees, the first three traits are nearly always reliably associated, and potential leaders tend to cluster at the extremes of these continua. That means the choice, human nature being what it is, is, as a rule, between leveling, careerist autocrats and egalitarian, mission-focused entrepreneurs. Moreover, once a preference for one or the other has been formed and become apparent in any given individual, usually quite early in life, the preference tends to be permanently fixed. On the other hand, leaders can often make changes in their place on the spectra of the last two traits—so one can hire for the first three (character) and train for the last two. Finally, the first three are the controversial traits: most of us readily agree that it is best to communicate well and inspire trust, respect, and confidence.

– 43 –
A Head to Head Comparison

Though this model does seem to capture much of what I am certain matters most to employee health and organizational productivity, I am not as confident as I would like to be that it, by itself, is likely to change the way we choose our administrators. When years of argument, study, and experience have failed to effect a change, and the hiring of entrepreneurial leaders seems to be decreasing, what can help those of us who hire or participate in hiring on teams and boards to appreciate that to retain success once it has been acquired, we must somehow get past or ignore the myths about machismo, rapacity, and ruling with an iron hand, about being cruel to be kind and doing more with less? What will teach us that these traits, however seductive in biographies, histories, novels, and movies, are less likely to bring success than misery to employees and mediocrity or catastrophe to firms? What will help us to understand that an autocrat is not preferable?

As mentioned previously, it is not possible to do a controlled experiment comparing different kinds of management. That is because no two workplaces are alike, and each can have only one leader at any one point in time. However, using our imaginations, it may be constructive to conduct a thought experiment to compare the two primary management styles head to head. That should give us the opportunity to make a broader and more detailed examination of the differences management styles can make and to obtain better insight into their impact. My goal here will be to provide as meaningful and balanced a story as possible and let you draw your own conclusions.

– 44 –

Case Study

We will examine a fictional division of a large pharmaceutical firm that has underperformed for ten years. It is a single site nonunionized mail order department comprised of thirty pharmacists, thirty pharmacy techs and thirty typists in a large rust belt city. It has had four managers in eight years and has been without one for the past two years. It is about to choose between an autocratic and an entrepreneurial leader. We will assume that each new manager starts in January and that the manager's management is supportive of the style of management in both cases; and we will follow the progress of each in parallel for eighteen months.

Autocratic	Entrepreneurial
Year 1	**Year 1**
January	**January**
New manager holds first general meeting: introduces himself and outlines his goals and expectations; there are going to be changes; will not tolerate laziness, bad behavior; long history of underperformance is going to end; will not hesitate to chastise, discipline, fire where appropriate; weekly meetings excessive and costly; from now on will call meetings as needed; asked how he will hear opinions, says make	New manager holds first general meeting: introduces herself; promises to listen and learn about problems; aware the site has a bad reputation; presumes that the workers present are not responsible for the reputation, that they are good employees and will try to help each one in achieving success for the organization; wants to learn what they think the problems are; open door policy; will always answer

an appointment during lunch on Thursdays and will be happy to listen as long as the comments seem constructive; can also send an e-mail, but e-mails take up a lot of his time, and so will answer only important e-mails, and may respond to the group as a whole.	e-mails; will be visiting, talking with, and working by the side of the various employees; she will try to be fair, will explain her reasons for all decisions and try to remove barriers and make work more pleasant for everyone; she does expect productivity to improve—that is what they are there for—but wants their help in reaching the goal; an employee draws attention to their mission statement: "Will provide high quality, cost-effective pharmaceuticals reliably, safely and efficiently and will help to advance the science of pharmacy;" says "management" focuses on efficiency and cost-effectiveness but not on safety or advancing science—suggests "they should either change the mission statement or address all of its components;" manager thanks him and says she will discuss this with her managers and bring the response to a later meeting; keeps the weekly meeting; adds once a month separate discipline meetings for the techs, the pharmacists, and the typists.
February	**February**
The site has been processing an average of 100 prescriptions a day per pharm tech; the company	The site average processing drops from 100 to ninety-five; the manager meets with each employee

average at their fifty other sites around the country is 110; the new expectation is 115 by the end of the year. Anyone not reaching this threshold will be fired.

Employees meet and send three representatives to present their concerns: two pharmacists and a pharm tech. Concerns mentioned: pressure to process without further support will lead to more errors and decrease the number of calls the pharmacists make to ordering providers; some other sites have hired a few clerks—would be helpful here; this site is #2 in narcotic prescriptions which take more time to process. Manager says he expects compliance without whining; he will not be dictated to: he fires one of the pharmacists and puts the other two "ring leaders" on probation.

individually, takes notes on meetings, identifies twenty concerns employees have and indicates she will work on top five first. Printers for each desk is the #1 concern (several called it a no-brainer)—walking down the hall to the central printer wastes time; they have been asking for this for years, but IT has refused, citing networking issues and what they see as a patent inefficiency. The new management makes the case, and by the end of March, every desk has a printer. Within a week, prescription average is back up to 102.

Another big concern is narcotic prescriptions; as this is complicated, the manager establishes a systems redesign team to address it. Six representatives will meet weekly for an hour in her office. There is a lot of bad behavior in what has been perceived as a permissive regime—long lunches, lots of time on the internet, and one employee who actually went out to a department store and bought shoes during working hours and bragged about it on Facebook. The shoe-buying employee was fired—the firing was explained and discussed at the weekly meeting; one of the typists said, "It's about

	time something was done," and there was prolonged spontaneous applause in response; new rules were made: anyone offsite in a nonemergency for more than fifteen minutes without prior permission would be subject to formal discipline. Five employees had such discipline.
March Hires a new quality manager to monitor efficiency; average has risen to 105 prescriptions per day, but annualized sick time average has increased from six days to nine days a year, and five pharmacists and three techs are known to be looking for new jobs; someone has contacted the Union and there is a meeting with employees planned for early June.	**March** The systems redesign team reports. It went beyond its brief and suggested that teams be set up—a pharmacist, tech, and typist would make up a team; that the teams could be in friendly competition and that some teams be devoted exclusively to narcotics; it is proposed that these narcotics teams be offsite in a secure facility (this facility has been raided twice in the past five years with substantial losses); there is a building across the street that is for rent and could serve; it was a bank in the past— the manager promises to pursue the question of the separate building, and, in the meantime, she introduces three dedicated narcotics teams.
April By now, thirty employees have been disciplined in a month—five are	**April** One particular pharmacist has been undermining the new manager,

out on extended sick leave with doctor's notes; the manager holds a meeting; he says that he thinks everyone is getting the message; efficiency has improved; behavior has been exemplary; they are on target for meeting the end of the year goal; replacements for two departed clerks are arriving next week; one pharmacist is being credentialed; he says: "Do not let the team down; put your back into the work; it's what you're paid for, and it's the right thing to do; if you start to listen to what I am telling you, we will all be happier and more successful."	agitating for her departure, suggesting that she is a wolf in sheep's clothing, making believe she is their friend but actually just trying to get them to work harder; he is well-liked by his colleagues and influential; he functioned as a leader when there was no manager; he has not concealed his comments and the manager has heard about them. She meets with him to give him his midyear evaluation: it reflects his good work as a pharmacist but also the negative impact he is having on the department; he is angry and intransigent; she suggests mediation; he insists on meeting with her manager, which is arranged; the meeting is surprisingly subdued, just a mild formal complaint, and then suddenly, a week later, he apologizes and becomes one of her most vocal supporters.
May	**May**
Quality manager creates a spreadsheet that compares the efficiency of the various employees. She brings in a consultant colleague to do a study of the activities and coordination of staff members and to educate staff on how to become more efficient; most productive employee of the month award is introduced; Connie Davis, a phar-	Negotiations for the building across the street begin; the three-member teams have been set up, and there is a good deal of enthusiasm; three one-hour team building sessions help to outline what teams can accomplish, and each team meets for one hour every other week to discuss problems and improve processes. As the teams get going, it

macist from an academic setting, applies for a job but is not hired—the manager feels that academics are sticklers for following protocol and inefficient.	becomes clear that cross coverage is inadequate, and they move to ten superteams of three teams each (one superteam is the narcotics team); by June, the non-narcotic teams are completing an average of 125 prescriptions per day and the narcotic teams eighty a day; employees are more cheerful and less stressed; absences have dropped; two techs and a pharmacist have left to follow their spouses to better jobs; one pharmacist who'd developed lung cancer retired; three typists have left as well; hiring for all open positions is in process.
June	**June**
A vote for the introduction of a union is set for this month; feelings run high; car windows are broken, the air is let out of tires; prank e-mails are common; a rumor begins to circulate that the new manager is having an affair; he holds another meeting at which he states that an up and down vote is fine with him; a union will not change his approach to management; it will just protect the worst workers and undermine the best, and if that's what they want, that's what they'll get; it will also increase their overhead so that they will have to work harder just	A new pharmacist, Connie Davis, who was in an academic setting before joining the department, meets with the manager to suggest that the facility should form a relationship with the local university; it would help with the research part of the mission; and teaching could keep pharmacists on their toes; the manager promises to look into it and asks whether the pharmacist has a contact; she does and provides the information; the contact refers the manager to the Pharmacy Program Director at the University, who indicates that the department is growing and that the training

to break even; three weeks before the vote, a legal opinion prevents it from taking place: the entire corporation would have to choose a union or not; one site, whatever its size, cannot unionize alone; the manager throws a party for the staff and brings pizza; the next week a female lab tech brings an EEO suit for sexual harassment by the manager.

program would love to set up student and resident rotations; they also have an active research program with funded projects, lots of ideas and training in statistics and how to develop research projects; he is enthusiastic about shared projects and suggests that the university could support her pharmacists to learn to develop and manage their own projects; a wide-ranging discussion as well touched on the fact that the engineering school had sent students for projects who had helped the University Pharmacy department to be more efficient; and he suggested work study programs.

July

Six of the original thirty pharmacists have taken other jobs, most of them at pharmacies in town; four pharmacy techs and three typists have gone as well, among them one Tom Smith, who has left to join a friend in a computer repair and refurbishing venture; and now eight employees are on extended sick leave (six with emotional problems, one with carpal tunnel dysfunction and one with back pain); one replacement pharmacist arrived in April and a second is due later in the month; the manager is advertising

July

Two weeks later, as soon as the minimal requirements have been met, two work-study students begin work; the more rigorous paperwork for the fulltime students and residents—development of curricula, meeting of requirements—is begun, along with the choosing and coaching of teachers; meetings to discuss research are established and a request for a half day a week free from prescription work for pharmacists to pursue approved research projects is forwarded to the central office; after a month

for two locums; two pharmacy techs have been hired, a third is on the way, and he has begun to contract with an outside typing service to cover for the absent typists; typists will no longer be replaced when they leave. There is a lot of concern among professional staff about the new typists—too many errors, poor communication, and slowness in response time have created delays in mailing drugs; the manager says that he expects the employees to train and support the new typists—however, the individuals assigned by typing service keep changing; average processing is now 111 per experienced tech, but the total number of prescriptions per day is down from 3000 to 2850 and they are going out more slowly; the manager explains to his boss that this reflects the turnover in employees and the "growing pains" related to the typing pool.	or two, however, a new mission statement is shared; the phrase about advancement of science has been removed; central office makes clear that it will not support research on company time and will not encourage research at all; the plans for the teaching program are approved though and an arrangement for one engineering project per semester is made—in this case, student and teacher will function as consultants for pursuing process improvement.
August	**August**
One of the most efficient pharmacy techs, someone the manager has publicly praised for being most productive of the month, suggests that they separate out narcotics because that is what slows them down most. The manager says that if they were staffed better, that	While working as a pharmacist, which she does every Monday, the manager realizes that it is not only narcotics that slow her down; while diabetes and hypertension meds go quickly, antipsychotics and anticoagulants, particularly Coumadin, slow her down because they

might be a good plan, but, as it was, it would make it harder for employees to cover one another and, with the high turnover in these professions and particularly in this geographic area, everyone must be ready, at the drop of a hat, to cover all aspects of the work.	require more cross-checking. She suggests at the next pharmacy discipline meeting that perhaps they could use a computer program to segment their prescriptions by category and time spent per prescription; using the time stamps and the categories, they can further divide the difficult from the easier and possibly carve out other "specialties" for teams to tackle; a new systems redesign team takes this on.
September The manager plans a two-day retreat for early December; it will take place at an attractive hotel in town and will begin one afternoon and end at noon the next day; he has arranged for another site to process their prescriptions during the retreat; they will be doing the same for the other site in November. (Anyone who would like overtime should sign up.) Though he has been working now for nearly a year, this will mark the true beginning for him as manager, he suggests. He will be rolling out his new program at the retreat.	**September** Because the prework is extensive, the academic rotations will not start until the new academic year; however, as part of their University rotations, residents have started to come a week at a time to do projects or give training sessions; a particularly good talk on new anticoagulants, associated with continuing education credit, was presented by one of them onsite during lunch and was attended by most of the staff; enough of those and it will not be necessary to send employees away for a week each year for training—and the training can be tailored to the needs of the pharmacists; they make suggestions—the next talk, on pain medications, is given by a well-known full pro-

<table>
<tr><td></td><td>fessor; the staff is impressed and excited.</td></tr>
<tr><td>October</td><td>October</td></tr>
<tr><td>A second sexual harassment EEO suit is filed. The lawyer for both women contacts the manager and leads the manager to understand that the suits were filed to protect the jobs both need. After talking with the company lawyer, the manager agrees to keep both techs on without pressuring them to perform in return for having the suits dropped.</td><td>The new systems redesign team reports; non-steroidal anti-inflammatory drugs (like ibuprofen), anticoagulants (like warfarin), and antipsychotic drugs (like haloperidol) take longer and become specialties—for cross-coverage purposes, each becomes the responsibility of one superteam; at first they simply channel all the prescriptions to the superteam and let that team decide how and when to process them. Then, because it turns out to be the most efficient strategy, a primary and a secondary team are formed, and they work on their drug specialty in the mornings, the secondary team doing regular work when the primary team cannot manage the entire volume.</td></tr>
<tr><td>November</td><td>November</td></tr>
<tr><td>Behind the scenes, the manager, speaking to his boss, expresses concerns about the quality of the workers he inherited; he feels that they had become lazy and resistant to change before he arrived, spoiled by coddling and bad management; he wants to bring in more efficient workers; he suggests that pharma-</td><td>A scandal erupts that makes the national news: five workers have been pilfering narcotics for years; they had of course tried to block the transition to having teams that process strictly narcotics; when they failed, even though two of them managed to get themselves assigned to the new teams, they had had to</td></tr>
</table>

cists are the key to success, and he would like to replace 80% of those that remain; they need a source and agree to work with an agency which places pharmacists that have had troubled histories—with credentialing, former employers, legal issues, or the like. Because they wish to reestablish themselves, they are willing to work in the rust belt for low pay; they are also willing to take direction—to make fewer contacts with physicians, for example, and so complete more prescriptions in a shorter time.	stop their lucrative practices; then, one of the university residents on project assignment to improve efficiency, reviewing the prior year's prescriptions, discovered the diversion; the student told the manager; the manager contacted the DEA; the DEA conducted a rapid undercover investigation; and the five were arrested one morning at nine AM; otherwise turnover has been minimal; hiring has become easier with the University providing help; however, as notice remains short, hiring takes time and getting up to speed takes more, the manager introduces gap positions, one for each discipline—they cover for turnover, and, when there is no turnover, for absences of more than a week—extended sick time, vacations, and the like. A pool of "substitutes" for each discipline is also developed for absence on short notice—especially same-day call-ins.
December The retreat begins with an inspirational speaker; then the manager presents what he calls the brutal facts (he has also read Good to Great and taken his own lessons); the site remains substandard, he says; despite his best efforts to help them achieve the satisfaction that goes	**December** The manager hosts a holiday party at a local hotel; there is a sit-down dinner and a band; 250 people attend; there is a short formal agenda at which the president of the company distributes awards and announces a substantial bonus for each employee; she thanks everyone

with a job well-done, the room is full of nay-sayers, lazybones, and rebellious teens; so, since they have not responded to low level discipline, the quality manager, or the consultants in the right spirit, a new day is dawning; anyone can ask for the help they need and they will receive it, but, if they are not completing 115 prescriptions a day, they will be subject to progressive discipline up to and including separation; they should all have learned prescribing efficiency at school; they are encouraged to request any remedial training they may need here on the job and we will try to provide it, but from now on, efficiency in handling prescriptions will be a basic job expectation, like recognizing drug names and pill appearances, like computer skills, using the telephone and typing; allowing you to continue to work at the present slow rate is allowing you to steal from our customers, our company, our stockholders; one highly functioning pharmacist, one of those he was planning to keep on, has a heart attack the next morning in the midst of a heated discussion during a coffee break, and he dies.	for the progress they have made during the year.

Year 2

March

Fifteen of the thirty original pharmacists are gone or on extended leave; three pharmacists had been hired through normal channels, and another ten had been acquired from the agency. Average prescriptions filled per tech were now 118 a day and, in fact, exceeding the national average; but average sick day use is up to eleven per year; two more employees have had heart attacks; three pharmacists and six techs are out on extended sick leave; two techs have settled for substantial annuities; so total prescriptions completed remain below average, and speed remains substandard; still management is happy with the progress at a site which had previously resisted every effort.

There are few smiles; most employees look at the floor and do their socializing behind closed doors, during lunch or breaks; some do still often sit and complain about how bad things are, sometimes for a half hour at a time; there are occasional explosions of anger, fights that rage out of control, but otherwise the workplace is quiet

Year 2

March

Three superteams have been short a typist; two of these teams have requested support, and the manager has supplied typists from a temp agency; the third team, though, has gone two weeks without asking for help and the manager asks why; it turns out that one of the remaining typists, one Tom Smith, is also a computer programmer and has developed a collection of short cuts, templates, and automated processes to complete the task in much less time; he has actually been acting as a receptionist for the team as well, placing calls and getting the doctors on the line for the pharmacist; in the past he has always kept these ideas and inventions to himself—he did not want his fellow workers to lose their jobs due to his innovations; but if they can begin to function as telephone and logistical support, they can stay on and increase efficiency; over the next six months, with the programmer/typist helping to perfect the processes and train the other employees, they are able to decrease the number of typists by twenty and create a new job so

and empties out precisely at 4:30; some employees are pleased with the change—they come to work, do their job and go home; the cliques are gone; the politics have died back; and they aren't constantly being told they are one of the worst sites in the system anymore.	that each superteam also has a receptionist/support worker. By this time, non-specialty teams are finishing 150 prescriptions, narcotic teams 100, and other specialties 140; they are leading the country in both speed and productivity. Many employees now arrive a half hour or forty-five minutes early: to set up, socialize, and get an early start, and the facility now doesn't empty out until six; everyone is always smiling.
April One disgruntled employee brings suit for wrongful discharge; she talks about her frustrations at length to anyone who will listen; a reporter does, and a long article, unfavorable to the company, appears in the local newspaper, linking this suit with others around the city and suggesting that since bad management is an unhappy fact of contemporary corporate life, workers need to find ways to cope; the company writes an exculpatory letter to the editor.	**April** The lease on the property across the street becomes available; a move is planned for May; narcotics will move there since it does provide greater security; and central office has also decided to close another site in a nearby rust belt city and transfer the operations: ten pharmacists, twelve techs and eight typists will be joining them; the local Chamber of Commerce gives the manager and her boss awards for their "high-quality management and contribution to the community" and Tom Smith, the typist-programmer is promoted and moves to national headquarters.
June Two malpractice suits are brought	**June** The pharmacists take the manag-

<table>
<tr>
<td>against the company for wrongful death; in one case, a patient taking Coumadin and three drugs that can interact with it had died; in the other a patient who had had three large narcotic prescriptions in a week, all processed at this site, had died of an overdose; in neither case had the pharmacist contacted the doctor to suggest a change in prescription; both pharmacists were agency acquisitions.</td>
<td>er out to dinner to recognize and thank her for her support and the things she has done to improve their circumstances and performance; they offer to help in any way they can.</td>
</tr>
<tr>
<td>

July

The manager tells his boss that he is interviewing for a new position with more responsibility and greater pay out West and asks for her support; she tries at first to keep him by increasing pay and perks—"you are the only one who has been able to get them to make even the smallest change"—then gets him to agree to stay until December to finish the transition and lets him write his own recommendation, which she reads from or paraphrases when HR representatives call to ask about him; the focus is on his success in this turnaround situation—he quickly brought a site on the ropes back to profitability.

</td>
<td>

July

The manager's boss evaluates her as above average; she has had a generally good eighteen months, but she's been lucky; the best ideas have come from some unusually capable workers; and she must accept that when she championed research, she embarrassed the company into changing its mission statement after twenty years and they were not happy; but if she pays careful attention to experience and advice, she will learn; she does seem to have a good attitude and is likely to do better next year; the manager offers to step down and become just a pharmacist again; when her offer is not accepted, she starts to prepare for the new trainees; and to think about how to deal with the influx of new em-

</td>
</tr>
</table>

<table>
<tr><td></td><td>ployees; should they form new teams or should the veteran teams be broken up so that the new folks can be distributed among the old teams; she will bring it to the general meeting next week; she hopes and expects that they will support distributing the new folks among the old teams.</td></tr>
</table>

I have never worked in or formally studied a mail order pharmacy, or any pharmacy for that matter, though I have worked with pharmacists; I have fabricated the statistical details, from the time required to process different categories of drugs, the numbers of employees and numbers of prescriptions per day to numbers of people changing jobs and out sick, out of whole cloth, though I have based my *"facts"* on real-world observations, discussions with pharmacists, my medical and management experience, and my impressions of probabilities. My goal has been to convey the global nature and impact of management styles by considering day-to-day operations.

– 45 –

Comments about Team Building

I'm sure you will draw your own conclusions, but there are a few observations that I think are worth making:

1. You probably noticed that the length of the monthly entries is often unequal. In part, that has to do with the nature

of each approach. The entrepreneur tends to spend more time at the start sharing ideas, forming relationships, and trying out different strategies. She is more open to creative suggestions. And she has introduced additional new projects and programs. So only once in the first eleven months is the entry for the autocrat longer than that of the entrepreneur. The autocrat doesn't spend time getting opinions or trying to convince people of the value of his plans. He just introduces them. Nor are they additional—they are replacements. Later, there is a tendency for problems to arise for the autocrat, created by his management style, which the entrepreneur will not face. Putting time into team-building at the start tends to prevent dissension later. So while the entrepreneur celebrates Christmas with a party, the autocrat is laying down the law.

2. Eighteen months is pretty early innings for team-building, but some benefits are often seen early. One mind tends to be less creative than a team, new ideas can come from anyone, and feedback from workers can help to keep managers on track when they are open to that feedback. The team that addressed narcotics and the suggestions from Connie Davis and Tom Smith are cases in point.

3. Entrepreneurs often get less support from their managers than autocrats do. Arranging with bosses to approach things as good cop-bad cop can be helpful—this lets the manager be her employees' representative. But that kind of arrangement requires a strong and insightful boss. Sometimes entrepreneurs are caught in the middle, not viewed as team players by their superiors, but viewed as sold out to their bosses by their reports. Their effectiveness depends on their ability to tell the truth most of the time, to deliver for their employees, and to have open communications with their bosses. The nature of the entrepreneur's

evaluation suggests that all is not well in her relationship with her boss.

4. Entrepreneurs focus on how to accommodate workers; autocrats tend to replace workers for tractability and loyalty. If a worker has a child starting school, an entrepreneur will likely ask whether the worker needs an accommodation to stay on. The worker might want to come in after dropping the child at work. Accommodations might be working through lunch or going part-time. The entrepreneur would try to arrange such options. The autocrat would probably never raise the question, would let the worker go, and hire someone *less needy*. Bosses often seem to put little emphasis on the impact of such different approaches, but employee replacement takes time. First, there is short-staffing, then temps, then a new hire, who needs training and experience on the job before being up to speed, and with the attendant risk that he may not work out. Once again, early effort saves time later.

A Broader Context

– 46 –

Applies at All Levels

So far I have been using the terms manager, boss, and leader indiscriminately, treating them as a class; making no distinction, for example, between managers and administrators—between the CEO of an international corporation employing 10,000 people and a manager of five clerks at one of that corporation's warehouses. I have made no distinction because I believe the principles that govern their value are the same at every level. Employees at every level have within them a desire to contribute their time and skills as completely as they possibly can, to be infinitely productive in the service of an enthusiastic and supportive manager in the pursuit of a worthy purpose. Helping them to find that commitment in themselves, to find the freedom that consists of, as Robert Frost so insightfully put it, *"moving easily in harness,"* is the job of all leaders at every level.

There may be a tendency to think, particularly among those who have always hired autocrats, that if they are going to try out this risky entrepreneurial leader idea, it might be best to introduce one in a mid-level management position but that a traditional autocrat is still best at the top. In fact, the drive to excel is, if anything, greater, the higher in an organization one inquires. An entrepreneurial manager will be more entrepreneurial and more effective with a supportive boss, someone who provides resources, discusses options and helps her find reserves of talent within herself. And, of course, the entrepreneurial CEO has a broader impact since she determines the working environment for the entire corporation, whatever the departmental microenvironments. And the management styles rarely mix fruitfully. An autocratic boss can certainly choose to be supportive of an entrepreneurial report, but he will never inspire the extraordinary performance that is in her; while a non-supportive autocrat can turn an entrepreneurial manager from one of your greatest assets into an unremarkable liability; and an autocratic supervisor can, in turn, nullify the efforts of her entrepreneurial boss, at least in her own sphere of influence. Taking a greater *risk* will generally bring a greater return. If a corporation plans to convert, as I suggest, to an entrepreneurial management style, the change, in nearly all cases, needs to be system-wide. Although clearly the change doesn't have to happen all at once; and it will probably be best to start as close to the top as possible.

– 47 –

Applies in Nearly All Circumstances

So far as well, I have only distinguished between startups and established corporations, though the department in my pharmacy case study was clearly in a turnaround state. Do the particular challenges a company might be facing demand different management styles? Might an autocrat be preferable to manage expansions, realignments, or maintenance situations; to manage bankruptcy, acquisitions, or downsizing? Here, my answer is somewhat less unconditional. Though once again, in most cases, the entrepreneur is more likely to be successful and achieve a greater degree of success in most common settings, it may take him somewhat longer. So, in the rare situation that a small success in a matter of days or weeks seems more important than a large success over months or years, an autocrat may be preferable. That aside, however, the same dynamics apply to achieving success in each stage of corporate development. Though the specific goals may differ, building an enthusiastic, flexible, and effective team, willing to follow a leader towards any goal that serves the mission is required in each case. A couple of representative examples may help illustrate the general principle.

One common scenario involves the startup that has succeeded far beyond its wildest dreams—a local company that achieves national distribution of, let's say, a pomegranate chocolate bar and now has that and five other products in supermarkets nationwide. The young woman who has achieved this success had no prior business experience, and so she sets out to learn more. She is convinced, at a seminar she attends, that her company is at the end of a growth spurt, and she decides to hire a couple of experts to improve her company's efficiency. She hires two recent MBA graduates, who, moderately autocratic, bring academic ideas about responsible and rational management to the day-to-day running of the business in order, they say, to optimize profits. They announce an immediate focus on developing existing accounts before any further expansion occurs, and "temporarily" cut funding of R&D in half to support the sales team. And, as with a dynamic football team that has built up a large first half lead and then plays a defensive game in the second half and nearly loses, at that point, the exponential growth stops, the organization becomes less fun to work for, and many of the most creative employees leave. The now more traditional company shows a growth in profits, attracts more conservative investors, and is said to be more realistic and more responsible than before. Had the founder maintained her instinctive entrepreneurial approach, however, the longer-term market share and profit margin might well have been orders of magnitude greater.

At first glance, it may seem most efficient and least expensive to manage realignment, restructuring or downsizing with an autocrat. However, if the goal is not to close permanently, these conversions are best managed with sensitivity, respect, understanding, and the participation of the workforce. Though the part of the workforce being reassigned or asked to leave is not likely to be pleased, it may be less litigious—and less liable to public criticism. Also, by limiting the trauma as it occurs, an entrepreneurial manager may limit its impact on the remaining workforce so that disruption is minimized, productivity suffers as little as possible, even in the short term, and recovery is swift. Corporate culture is extremely sensitive to what happens to employees, but also to how it happens and who is accountable. In the absence of accurate information, paranoid rumors circulate; and an us-and-them gap, if it does not already exist, can be rapidly established between workers and management, precisely when as much harmony as possible is desirable. Autocrats tend to exacerbate such paranoia and so can elicit a less attractive outcome.

– 48 –
Applies to Impresarios

If asked who they would like to be managed by, few people would hesitate to choose entrepreneurial managers. Yet when the same people are choosing managers to lead their organizations, with a focus on how to extract the greatest productivity from their workforce and an anxiety about being too soft, too idealistic, too slow or impractical, they often choose autocrats. An impression that hiring the ruthless and the greedy, those determined to succeed at any cost is the best way to achieve market domination, has been extraordinarily persistent.

It is likely that this notion stems from the prevalent belief that the enlightened self-interest of individuals investing to gain the maximum return, that greed, creates the greatest wealth. There is widespread admiration for, and envy of, the robber barons, for Andrew Carnegie, John D. Rockefeller, Cornelius Vanderbilt and Henry Ford; for tough inflexible sports coaches, forever demanding pushups and wind sprints; for the marine sergeants who preside over basic training; and even for pirates and gunslingers and Vikings and Nazis—for *forces of nature*, those who let nothing get in their way, get things done, and reap outsized rewards. And there is a similar feeling about contemporary Silicon Valley successes: for the entrepreneurs who built Microsoft, Facebook, Google, Amazon, Yahoo, and Apple. In the words of pertinent clichés, you have to be tough (and sometimes hated) to succeed; you may have to break a few eggs; it is important to stand tall and stick to your guns.

It can be argued, however, that though the CEOs of the new technology firms do become celebrities and can be uncompromising and arbitrary, even Mark Zuckerberg and Bill

Gates, known for their ruthlessness and competitive nature, are probably, on balance, far more entrepreneurial and less autocratic than the old robber barons. One important measure might be that when one focuses on the workplaces that have created these contemporary successes, they are not the traditional ones. Google has been, for most employees at least, not a salt mine but a playground or a carnival. People want to work there because they are treated so well. Employees at Microsoft and Facebook also have positive things to say about their workplaces—these are not the sweatshops of the 1800s. In any case, as discussed earlier, the leaders of startups may not all be appropriate models for hiring leaders for established firms. (In all likelihood, learning to kill and fight wars is not the best model either.) The leaders of startups choose themselves, and their employees often opt to work specifically for them. Moreover, it stands to reason that their success is generally more a function of a good business idea and plan, a new niche, a small number of high-quality employees, timing, and/or the absence of significant competition than of management style; and no matter how well they actually do, it can always be argued that their businesses might have fared better (or worse) under an entrepreneur than an autocrat.

– 49 –

Applies across the Board

If we are not seeking the new incarnation of a robber baron or even an accomplished present-day technology CEO, what are we looking for? Because it is easier to hire an entrepreneurial leader if you have a few examples in mind, I have devoted considerable effort to pinpointing some prominent representative individuals. However, most of the candidates that come immediately to mind are, for various reasons, flawed examples for our purposes. Martin Luther King, Mahatma Gandhi, and even Mother Teresa all seem to have been vigorous self-promoters (part of the reason we know them today) and are said to have often been difficult and uncommunicative with followers. Abraham Lincoln, a better model, was perhaps more isolated than one might desire in such a leader, and he is pretty much one of a kind. George Washington, though, particularly as he is presented in Ron Chernow's 2010 biography, does exemplify most of the traits we have defined as desirable and can therefore help us to understand and identify entrepreneurial leaders. He was demanding, but he was good at selecting, and he trusted, respected, and supported his direct reports, rewarded them for exertion and initiative and saw to their development and promotion; as Commander-in-Chief of the Continental Army, he shared the risks and misery of his soldiers; and he most often shared credit with others for success, while taking responsibility for failure. He is famous for not having been corrupted by power, and never unduly traded on his fame: he deferred to civilian authority, met with his generals to determine policy and was influenced by their input and opinions; and, far from enriching himself, he refused his salaries on principle and to his patent detriment, risked his home, fortune, and life for the mission he joined reluctantly, and surrendered solvency along with his dreams of creating a model plantation when he left for the Continental Congress in 1775. In private life, he was competitive and clumsy, ambitious for land, money, and slaves; and he had the contempt of landed gentry for the common worker. However, once he became a public figure, he devoted every resource he had to the mission of building a new nation and subordinated his personal inclinations and wishes to that goal, in the Army, at the Continental Congress, and as President; and his inclinations changed, so that, for example, he came to admire the common soldiers he had once despised. Franklin Delano Roosevelt, Dwight D. Eisenhower, and Michael Bloomberg seem to have exhibited some of the same entrepreneurial attributes in their public political lives. And yet, it is rather obvious that these examples are social or political personalities, while the robber barons and Silicon Valley founders are gloriously commercial and come much more readily to mind as models of autocracy.

There are companies that are said to preferentially choose servant leaders—Southwest Airlines, Medtronic, and American Family Life Insurance are examples. But of course, knowing that does not help one to recognize specific candidates for your workplace. Nor are there many prominent fictional or quasi-fictional biographical characters in this mold: biblical Solomon, perhaps; Jimmy Stewart's characters in *Mr. Smith Goes to Washington* and *It's a Wonderful Life*; the teacher played by Sidney Poitier in *To Sir with Love*, Robin Williams in *Dead Poets' Society*, Richard Dreyfus in *Mr. Holland's Opus*, Shirley MacLaine in *Madame Souzatzka*, Edward James Olmos in *Stand and Deliver*, Michelle Pfeiffer in *Dangerous Minds*, Bing Crosby in *Going My Way*; Luke Skywalker in *Star Wars*, Bilbo and Frodo in *The Hobbit* and *The Lord of the Rings*; Oskar Schindler as depicted in *Schindler's List*. Billy Beane, the character Brad Pitt plays in *Moneyball*, may be the most compelling such representation in film so far—he succeeds in a highly competitive business in a truly entrepreneurial fashion. What most, if not all, of these individuals have in common is some degree of humility, pertinent background acquired, apparently not by design but by chance, and some degree of surprise at finding themselves in an important role and actually being good at it. To take our search for models a step further, let's shift our focus from argument to narrative and indulge in a brief excursion into summer camp and ice cream.

A Brief Excursion: Summer Camp and Ice Cream

– 50 –

Summer Camp

It can be disorienting to look back at remote experiences from a privileged new vantage. When I was spending three high school summer vacations as a sports counselor-in-training, junior counselor and counselor at a summer camp, Buck's Rock Work Camp in New Milford, CT, I didn't concern myself much with its history or meaning for its founders. I did know that the camp was the creation of Ernst and Ilse Bulova, refugees from Nazi Germany. That it may well have represented their critique of, and proposed alternative to, that society, I only realized in retrospect. I have also come to understand that its name reflected its beginnings: the work camp began with a construction crew whose first assignment was building the living and dining spaces for what became a farm to help the war effort. Then, once the war was won, the construction crew built shops, studios and performance spaces for a camp that was increasingly devoted to child development through productive involvement in the visual, written, and performing arts. Over time, that has grown to include, according to the official history, printing, book making, glassblowing, lamp-working, woodworking, sculpture, painting, drawing, weaving, sewing, ceramics, batik, and jewelry; newspaper, magazine; and instrumental and vocal music, clowning and improv, theater, dance, video, music recording, and technical theater. The Bulovas, I have learned, had trained with Maria Montessori, but they had their own approach to optimizing children's education. They therefore not only interviewed the counselors but also each prospective camper, with the goal of creating a dynamic but stable community, one where everyone could grow and learn. And my place in their grand scheme was as a sports counselor. It was as if I was an apprentice at a garden variety sports camp, but with full access to a camp devoted to the arts next door.

Buck's Rock was where I first heard madrigals, the blues, and chamber music performed; where I first saw *The Madwoman of Chaillot* and met with intellectual pomposity and arrogance. I recall using a paintbrush to coat palings with creosote and digging postholes for a fence. I remember cleaning out brush. I remember sitting around a table *"horse trading"* campers, choosing softball teams for the Watermelon League, a mere sixteen-year-old, negotiating, quite successfully, with three mature counselors for a competitive edge. I remember that I chose difficult campers, with reputations for innate talent but an inability to use it; and that my teams won when I helped those campers, one in particular who pitched and hit the long ball, to gain control. So I guess I was already a fledging entrepreneurial manager back then; and part of the camp milieu that created growth. The Bulovas could not have anticipated what specifically I would do for good or ill when they chose me; I doubt they ever knew. But choosing me did work, as far as I can see.

Ernst left a final statement just before he died at ninety-eight. In it, he said: "I believed in you. I believed in the millions of men, the millions of women who have lived, who are living now, who have ever lived. I know they were, they are, they will be vulnerable, threatened by death and injuries, accident and fate. But they were, they are, they will be endowed with eyes to see, with ears to hear, with brains to think, with hearts to feel. Growing, creating, spending their energies, deciding, choosing their roads." I don't think of Ernst and Ilse Bulova as models of entrepreneurial business management. Their model *was* successful, and the camp has lasted now for seventy years, but it did not obviously outperform. It was and is prodigiously productive, but there is no accepted yardstick by which to measure its success.

Of course I met many people there as well: a girlfriend; a group that met during the school year in Great Neck on Long Island; one who went to college with me; and one in particular, a counselor in the jewelry shop, struck me as a kindred spirit, and we became friends there one summer. He threw pots and played the mandolin, and, delighting in one another's company, we were constantly together during our time off. I recall in particular sitting on benches about the grounds, singing, reading aloud from Carl Sandburg, discussing our interests and the state of the world. I remember him as quiet, thoughtful, unrushed, and uncertain, but also untroubled about the future. He liked what he was doing at that time, and that seemed to be enough; though he did have an energy and restlessness about him at times as well. Once or twice, I think, I visited him during the school year. I was a Good Humor man for about two weeks one summer, and, by chance, his house was on my route. Though we got along well whenever we were together, we gradually lost touch—as I did with many high school and college friends and people I met from all walks of life over the years.

– 51 –

Bud's

Four years later, I started medical school at the University of California at Davis. Sometime during that first year, our Nutrition professor told us that a banana split makes a good balanced meal, and, as I had no problem at that time of life with weight, I took to going to Dairy Queen near the railway station for a banana split lunch once a week. A good college friend had moved to the Noe Valley section of San Francisco before I arrived. I visited him often, and among the many things we did together was to stroll the couple of blocks from his apartment to stand in line for an ice cream that seemed to us well worth the wait.

Before that, as I was growing up, like most of us a pretty big ice cream fan, my choices were vanilla, chocolate, strawberry, butter pecan, and a very green but not very tasty pistachio; oh, and, in some providential places in New England, various versions of maple walnut. My family bought most of our ice cream in gallons from the grocery store. In those days I had a greater focus on quantity than quality, though I was aware that, in the vanilla from Breyer's, you could see flecks of black (the vanilla bean, it was said) and that that ice cream did seem to taste better than other vanillas. The concept of premium or specialty or homemade ice cream, if it existed, had not yet entered my consciousness at that time.

My friend and I stood in line then to get into Bud's: as I remember it, a cramped storefront with a couple of freezers containing premium ice creams. I believe I liked the pistachio and that it was white rather than green. I know that the flavors were intense and exotic, the ice cream was creamier, and eating it was like eating ice cream cubed, the new and improved model. As the waits averaged forty-five minutes, there was lots of time to talk about how this might be, in this minuscule storefront on this neighborhood street in the Noe Valley, the best ice cream on the planet. We waited in line together like this perhaps five times altogether, but, they did leave behind an aura of enjoyment and delight before, like most good things, our visits came to an end. It was the early 1970s then. I left for Boston in 1975 and stayed on and off until 1977. I lost touch with this friend, too, over the years and never did get back to Bud's.

– 52 –

Steve's

And then, in Boston, I heard about Steve's, said to be a great ice cream place in Somerville. I was by then an intern and had little time off. Somerville was rather out of the way. So, like Bud's, Steve's was modestly inaccessible—I had to make a significant effort to get there. I finally did go with friends, though, two or three times, and it was another revelation—ice cream nearly as good as Bud's but with another advantage. Here you could get nearly anything "*smooshed in.*" I had always preferred my ice cream with nuts, and that had limited my choice of flavors. Now, not only had the flavors multiplied, but I could put the nuts of my preference in any of them. This even transformed for me the humble vanilla, chocolate, and strawberry—with walnuts or almonds, cashews or hazelnuts, they were new flavors.

– 53 –

Herrell's

Though I missed its early development, I finally caught up with Baskin Robbins across from Kapiolani Hospital in Honolulu, during my residency training. During my OBGYN rotation there, it took the place of my visits to Dairy Queen; I walked over and had a four by four (one of their sundaes) most days for lunch. Though their ice cream was not quite the quality of Bud's or Steve's, it was far better than what I had grown up with. I also met my wife, also an ice cream enthusiast, later that year in Honolulu—in the CCU over the heart monitors at Kuakini Hospital. For a while, at least, it was easy to find a Baskin Robbins nearly anywhere we went: Iowa to begin with, Seattle and the Northeast on vacation. But, by the time we returned to San Francisco in 1981, Bud's had been sold, and the store was gone; and by the time we returned to Massachusetts in 1983, Steve's had been sold as well. I had taken a job with a medical group in Amherst, Massachusetts, where there was also a Baskin Robbins, though, as it turned out, we almost never visited during the twenty years we were there. That was because we were surprised and pleased to discover there was a premium ice cream parlor in downtown Northampton, around the corner from the Academy of Music in Thorne's Marketplace—a parlor called Herrell's. The ice cream was once again extraordinary, the equal of that at Bud's and Steve's. It turned out that *that* was because it *was* Steve's. The story we heard then was that Steve Herrell, who had founded Steve's, had decided to move to San Francisco. He sold his business and the name Steve's to a corporation and started West; he spent the first night with friends in Northampton, loved it, and never left. I later read that he had a two-year noncompetition agreement and worked those two years as a piano tuner. I never got to ask him what of that was true, but Herrell's celebrated its fortieth anniversary in Northampton three years ago. Then, in 2007, having moved back to California for work, during a visit to Monterey, we discovered, on Fisherman's Wharf, a sign in a shop window that claimed it was selling Bud's ice cream. It was not quite as I remembered it, but it *was* a good premium ice cream.

– 54 –

Ben and Jerry's

It was in the 1980s that we began to hear about Ben and Jerry's ice cream. By then, we had discovered Emack and Bolio's in Boston, arguably the best ice cream I ever tasted. We were always willing to try something new, but for quite a while we didn't happen upon any of Ben and Jerry's parlors; and it was years before we eventually went to their headquarters in northern Vermont on a trip to the Montreal Film Festival. One day in a supermarket, though, I did see quarts of their ice cream on sale, and I noticed a picture of the founders on the cover. It turned out that Ben was Bennett Cohen, my friend from Buck's Rock during high school. We talked once, briefly on the telephone in the late 1980s or early 1990s. By then Ben and Jerry's, unlike Steve's or Bud's, had become a household name, part of the culture; and Ben himself was a public figure.

He was an ice cream man with his own route after I was; he continued for years to throw pots and did some teaching before he and Jerry got their start in ice cream. The legend says that they were planning on bagels first, but that the equipment was too expensive. His road to management was certainly haphazard, but his predispositions and experiences had given him the skills to do it well. There is no way I can prove this, but I am certain that had he been recognized and hired back when he was an ice cream man or an obscure potter in a small town in New England, to manage a grocery store, a clothing factory, a computer startup, or a human resources department, he would have been a runaway success. Of course, someone would have had to encourage him to apply, to choose and support him; he would not have pursued such opportunities on his own. Fortunately, he and a partner had the skill, vision and courage to start their own wildly successful business. Still, I suspect that a prior stint as a manager might have decreased their anxiety and increased their confidence as they started out. With Jerry, he has shared his philosophy of management in *How to Run a Values-Led Business and Make Money, Too* and various other publications and commentaries online.

Although he was the leader of a startup, from what I can tell, once he had achieved his initial success, he turned out to be a useful model, the kind of individual who makes a good entrepreneurial manager. He was flexible and practical; he treated his employees well; he was humble and willing to take advice; he did not seek fame or great wealth—they found him; he was inspirational and communicated well; he clearly behaved as if anything worth doing is worth doing well; though he would never have made a thing of it back then, his pots and his jewelry were inventive and attractive, and he played the mandolin extremely well.

– 55 –

Some Updates

I learned just recently that when Bud's began to sell premium ice cream and gained its success and reputation, it was no longer owned by Bud Scheidelman. Alvin Edlin, his cousin, bought the creamery business from him in 1952. It was Alvin who developed the premium product, built the business and then sold it in 1980 for enough money to retire. The Bud's ice cream we discovered in Monterey in 2007 was made by Berkeley Farms, a creamery that had bought the business and moved in 1998 from Emeryville to Hayward in California's Castro Valley. It has subcontracted as well to a company in Bangkok that has created a successful chain of Bud's ice cream parlors in Southeast Asia, presumably surprising and delighting many Thais today, as Bud's once, more than forty years ago now, delighted me. Though I must admit I have no idea what any of their management styles were.

Steve sold Steve's in 1977 to Joe Crugnale, who later founded Bertucci's and resold Steve's in 1983. It was then widely "*co-located*" with the D'Angelo's chain of subs at sites all over the Eastern seaboard. From the outside, this did not seem like a good business plan, since D'Angelo's was a lot like Subway—more fast food than specialty, and so the concurrence or crossover of customers was not likely to be large. More importantly, when we visited one of the sites in western Massachusetts, to our taste, the quality had dropped—either the quality control was deficient, or cost control had had an impact on the ingredients. In any case, the chain never did very well, and it closed in the 1990s after another acquisition. Recently one of the original employees from the Somerville store bought the rights to

Steve's, opened in Brooklyn, and has begun to expand.

For forty years, Steve Herrell has had his new successful business in Northampton. He opened a franchise in Harvard Square in 1980 and another in Allston in 1984, but the business remained small, clearly his preference. His ideas and businesses trained and inspired others. Gus Rancatore, who started with Steve in Somerville, later founded first Toscanini's and, then, Rancatores', both successful ventures. Ben and Jerry said that he helped inspire them and get them started. He created the idea of smoosh-ins (now called by others mix-ins), the acknowledged foundation of Cold Stone Creamery's business model. He too has a reputation for treating employees well and has demonstrated an extraordinary business sense without formal business training.

There is a Ben and Jerry's now five minutes from our house In Eugene, Oregon, and we have visited from time to time, in part at least from a sense of nostalgia. But we have also taken to going to two local premium ice cream stores, though they are more remote and less architecturally attractive.

– 56 –

Some Implications

Most towns can sustain an ice cream parlor or two, and many have. There are legendary ice cream establishments in many cities; many of them produced home-made or premium ice cream without fanfare or larger ambition, and a few still do. Newer and even more exotic parlors continue to be developed. A comprehensive history of the ice cream industry might well be engrossing, but that is a vast story waiting to be told by another author in another time and place. Here there is only room for this short tour of my own experience, primarily an opportunity to entertain you and to set before you the example of Ben Cohen, who, with Jerry Greenfield, chose to expand from the ice cream parlor into the grocery store and built an ice cream empire, fought a David and Goliath war with Haagen-Dazs/Pillsbury (for grocery store shelf space) and won, and was named U.S. Small Business Person of the Year by President Reagan. He and Jerry chose to donate 7.5% of annual company pretax income to charitable causes, more than any other publicly traded corporation. They agreed that no employee, including the CEO, would have a salary more than five times that of any other. They held a free summer movie festival where they started in Burlington, VT, and gave away their ice cream for free one day each year. They used non-traditional marketing techniques, and their stock prices rose steadily for about ten years after they sold stock to Vermont residents during 1984 at public meetings. They made corporate profit only one third of their mission; that was accompanied by social responsibility and responsibility to its employees for their welfare and career growth. More detail is available, as noted earlier, in books and articles, online and in bookstores. Whatever one may think of their social program, it looks like beating the competition with one hand tied behind your back. In a world where 90% of businesses fail, and competition is fierce, Ben Cohen and Steve Herrell are heartening models of entrepreneurial management success.

– 57 –

Concluding the Excursion

The best managers are like Ben. To the extent that they are greedy, that greed is tempered by altruism or by an understanding that success is built upon a satisfied team of workers and motivated by a mission that involves more than money. You might argue that you cannot hire a Steve Herrell or a Ben Cohen, but I'd like to suggest again that you can when they are starting out, if you can identify them as worthy and offer them the opportunity to pursue their dreams in the work you offer them. The energy and the passion is in them, and it can be harnessed to create outsized success. Perhaps your HR department should be canvassing individuals taking small business courses; or you may have a Steve or a Ben languishing in an entry-level job and ready to leave because he or she doesn't face any stimulating challenges. And it pays to take advantage of the placements that schools, in particular business schools, may make available despite the frustrations often associated. As with employees at all levels, it is wise to hire for character—in the case of managers, for independence, intelligence, responsibility, creativity, altruism, and ambition. It need not be career or economic ambition, but it should be an ambition to excel, to make it into the best possible situation, the situation in which they are placed.

A Few Last Issues

– 58 –

A Manager's Tenure

How long should you expect a manager to stay in a given position? How long would you like her to? These questions are easy to answer when the manager is unsuccessful (you'd prefer an immediate departure), when there was an agreement in advance, and when the job involves the achievement of a specific goal or completion of a task. However, most hires are open-ended; and most contracts allow either party to terminate the contract on relatively short notice. How long is best? And if it should end, how should it end?

It is not always easy to find a good manager, and transitions can be costly. It is generally difficult to replace satisfactory managers with individuals of equal caliber, and there is an interim of uncertainty, the honeymoon nearly always outweighed by the need to get up to speed, when productivity will usually drop, at least temporarily. For an entrepreneurial manager, making sure the department is fully successful can take quite a while, and the relationships formed in the process are often valuable and hard to recreate. Moreover, such managers have little drive to repeat the same kind of development in a new place—to be ready to leave, they will generally need to run out of significant tasks to accomplish or be tempted by new challenges.

Taking all this into account, any manager is likely to make his largest contribution in three to seven years. If new challenges continue to arise due to changes in mission, growth, or new tasks to accomplish—acquisition, new line of business or the like—that period could extend indefinitely, but in most workplaces, a leader will have optimized a department's functioning to the best of his ability in about five years. A change at that point is likely to be best for both company and manager, each remaining more productive than they would have been if the manager had stayed—especially if the manager is promoted.

When it is decided that a manager is to depart, the manager and his boss should meet, at least a year in advance, to discuss what is best for the department, what are the new and outstanding goals, what are the options to achieve them, what kind of person might manage best. Ideally, an agreement can be reached, a plan evolved, and a successor chosen so that an ample overlap will allow the departing manager to train the new and keep the impact of the transition on productivity to a minimum while making the transition relatively smooth and painless.

In fact, the orientation of a manager to the department, circumstances and needs, computer programs or uses new to her, and to the organization and its ways and culture if hired from outside, should also include a module devoted to management and promotion. From day one, the manager's boss should have her development in mind and arrange involvement in appropriate organizational or outside degree or non-degree leadership and skills development programs, and in appropriate formal and informal industry groups, societies and boards. Hiring the best people, trusting but observing and testing them, training and developing them, and helping and encouraging them to build successful careers is the best path to an organization's success. The number of employees promoted within and outside the organization should be an important part of the evaluation of a manager. A reputation for support and development will attract the best new candidates to apply for positions, and it brings out the best in those working for you every day.

– 59 –

The Most Important Manager

In any organization, because she defines the overarching culture and vision, it is likely that the second most important person you will hire is your CEO. But the most important may be less obvious: that is your manager of Human Resources. Because it is a support department, is not engaged in the company's primary business, and does not have direct contact with the company's customers, there is a tendency to provide it with fewer resources, operate a few employees short, and accommodate a manager you would never dream of in the more rigorous parts of the organization. However, if you believe that the quality of the people you recruit and hire determines the quality of your organization and its success, that people are your most important resource, you will want a dynamic, world-class Human Resources department and will put ample means at their disposal. A good HR manager will not only return your initial investment by making your HR operations more efficient and productive; she will also return that investment many times over by identifying and helping to hire and retain quality people, weeding out problems, and never letting the best candidates slip away.

– 60 –

Inside or Out

If you have until now chosen autocratic managers and plan to hire entrepreneurs this time around, you will almost certainly want to hire from outside the firm. Autocracy can give rise to fear, anger or resentment in, and sets a bad example for, employees, and that can make it difficult for them to bring the necessary enthusiasm, objectivity and clearness of vision to the management of your department—you may be lucky enough to find a Nelson Mandela among them, but other less constructive reactions are far more common. In time, though, the goal should be to hire most of the time from within. From time to time, an outside perspective may still be salutary, but the maintenance of a successful corporate culture, continuity and lower cost, and the creation of opportunities for your own employees to advance are arguments for internal hiring.

If you do choose to hire from outside, I would suggest that you be creative and comprehensive in your identification of candidates, but vet them through a ruthless and conventional sieve. It is generally better to try a second or third time to identify high-quality candidates than to compromise and hire someone who does not have the character you seek or to take a flyer on someone who looks good on paper and just might work out. Bring the promising candidates for onsite interviews; make sure a broad range of employees from HR, from all levels of the department, and from administration is involved; and gather everyone's opinion, from secretary to CEO, in writing, preferably using a high-quality HR instrument and then, if possible, at an open meeting, held within forty-eight hours of the interview. In the end, though, the final decision should be made by the person who will be the new manager's supervisor. If the supervisor is to be held responsible for the department's growth and welfare, she must have the opportunity to choose the employees that will make them possible. Good managers, however, are almost certain to appreciate the resources to facilitate timely identification, data gathering, and a diversity of opinions about candidates.

When hiring from within, one has the advantage of knowing a good deal about the candidates. It is relatively easy to identify those who communicate well and inspire respect, trust and confidence. One can also learn a good deal about attitudes toward management and encourage the entrepreneurial style in those who seem to be predisposed by precept and example. Earlier, I said, "Professional employees prefer someone with experience in the work he will be managing, if possible with long and distinguished experience, and ideally with some special insight into the work." I meant that hiring a chemist to manage physicists or a computer specialist to manage engineering is likely to create an insurmountable challenge. However, in many organizations, administrative/budgetary leaders serve beside the professional leaders, and in many areas, the skills required are more general and can be taught if necessary. Because the best entrepreneurial leaders often have unconventional backgrounds, it is useful to evaluate CVs carefully: alternative experiences, as treasurers, secretaries, or presidents of organizations, captains of sports teams, as teachers or inventors, and praise from coworkers that suggests unusual insight, skill, or helpfulness should be weighed along with degrees and corporate experience. When hiring internally, it is generally preferable to choose a leader who has stood out as a contributor to success, someone who, for example, makes insightful comments and proposals at meetings but does not blow his own horn or irritate his fellow workers, perhaps a little awkward or standoffish, but appreciated; not just *one of the guys*, not, that is, likely to go on socializing with them at and outside work or to have predefined favorites.

For the most crucial hires, whether from within or without, it is best to look in particular for those who have overcome significant adversity cheerfully, those who have built modules, managed projects, trained new employees, and had improbable successes. All things being equal, a thoughtful late starter in mid-career is often preferable to a conventional go-getter who has risen quickly and talks the talk. Although, as noted earlier, many entrepreneurial leaders prefer new challenges when they change jobs because they are loyal and focused on the mission of the organization that employs them, they can sometimes be prevailed upon to repeat a previous success in the same or a new organization. If you want to turn around a department, it can be expedient to hire an entrepreneurial leader who has successfully turned around a similar department. Still, each situation is, to some extent, unique and so will require a somewhat different approach to hiring.

– 61 –

Conclusion

I worked with someone at the Veterans Administration who had come up through the ranks. She had begun her career as an entry-level clerk fifteen years earlier and was now the Chief of Business Administration, a colleague with whom I got along well. We worked together on projects and had a standing monthly meeting to address the issues common to our departments. She shared anecdotes about the frustrations of her earlier years, the unfairness she faced, and her struggle to participate in decision-making; now she was supportive, even protective of her workers. I still recall vividly, though, the day I suggested to her that we managers should allow our employees to evaluate us. She said, without hesitation, that she would never stand for that; that she would run the department the way she wanted and did not want their input unless she asked for it for a limited particular purpose. She had had a long struggle to get to where she was, and she was not going to compromise any of her prerogatives now.

Autocracy is insidious. Power often does corrupt, even the good and well-intentioned among us—particularly those who seek power for its rewards, but also those who feel that they have, by the sweat of their brow, earned relief from some of their responsibilities due to the demands and importance of others. It is easy to simply accept such self-promotion as an inescapable aspect of human nature: man is imperfect and so we must take what we can get in the way of entrepreneurial leadership. This, however, readily becomes a slippery slope. Before we know it, trusting to instinct, we can end up back at autocratic leadership. We may find ourselves feeling autocracy is inevitable or explaining our distaste for the messy entrepreneurial model again. "A little too socialistic for my taste anyway;" "Leaders should look and act like leaders, should defer to their superiors, and should toe the line;" "Work is not a playground; it is critical and rigorous, and we are playing for keeps every day." Such arguments may be a real comfort; why not give up trying to find the elusive entrepreneurial manager and forget about trying to make this change? I would say because there is too much at stake—for you and for all of us.

To begin at a macroeconomic level, what might an autocratic to entrepreneurial change mean? It might not only result in higher stock prices, indices, and GDP, a smaller deficit, a much larger labor force participation rate (at the moment at its lowest point in thirty-five years), more tax dollars, more disposable income, more money for charitable donation, but also in a happier, healthier, more skillful, more optimistic, more productive workforce and population, new, innovative products, fewer mistakes, more cheerful, attentive, higher quality service everywhere we go: at the post office, the grocery store, the doctor's office, the motor vehicle bureau, the used car lot; fewer mistakes. We can only speculate about how this might change our feelings about our society and about life in general, but such a change would certainly promote many of the values we most cherish: health and wealth, life, liberty, and the pursuit of happiness and almost certainly improve personal, professional and social relationships throughout our society.

Back at the level of microeconomics, recognizing how it takes an unusual degree of insight and effort to make a start, getting out ahead of the curve, hiring entrepreneurs tomorrow, next week, next month, or next year will help your firm to a larger relative business success while creating a healthier more effective, more satisfied workforce, and a more cheerful workplace. Like monarchy and slavery, autocracy in the workplace has both moral and practical dimensions. In this case, we have just begun to identify the issue and have yet to come to grips with its impact on employees and productivity. Employee abuse is still acceptable and, in some circles, admired. We still place an irrational faith in this institution that clearly does not work and does extensive and irreparable harm. Perhaps this discussion will help us to begin to move in a more fruitful direction, to hire entrepreneurial managers and improve the lives of employees and the health and prosperity of our institutions.

Acknowledgements

Roberta Ruimy, Susan Roberts, Jian Huang, Ron Peters and my mother, Marilyn Cohen, for reading, commenting and suggesting revisions.

About Atmosphere Press

Founded in 2015, Atmosphere Press was built on the principles of Honesty, Transparency, Professionalism, Kindness, and Making Your Book Awesome. As an ethical and author-friendly hybrid press, we stay true to that founding mission today.

If you're a reader, enter our giveaway for a free book here:

SCAN TO ENTER
BOOK GIVEAWAY

If you're a writer, submit your manuscript for consideration here:

SCAN TO SUBMIT
MANUSCRIPT

And always feel free to visit Atmosphere Press and our authors online at atmospherepress.com. See you there soon!

About the Author

Alan Cohen had a satisfying career in medicine. Prior to retirement, he was a primary care doctor, a teacher, a manager, and a medical school administrator. He has also been a writer all his life, has been published in *The New England Journal of Medicine*, *The American Journal of Medicine*, *The New Yorker*, and *Poetry Magazine*, and has had many of his poems published in a variety of venues. He lives a full life with Anita, his wife of 44 years, most recently in Eugene, Oregon. He remains energetic, optimistic and hopes you find this book useful.

www.ingramcontent.com/pod-product-compliance
Lightning Source LLC
Chambersburg PA
CBHW062217150726
47991CB00006B/2323